a Time for Truth

"This book is a mosaic of glittering gems straight from the heart of one of the greatest expository preachers in the history of the evangelical church. This is a timely book with the ring of truth. Read it and be changed!"

Timothy George
Dean, Beeson Divinity School
Samford University

"*A Time for Truth* focuses upon life's inescapable problems. Dr. Olford's fruitful international ministry, his skill in Biblical exposition, and his unique communication gifts have produced a fountain of practical wisdom, reading pleasure, and spiritual insight. *A Time for Truth* is 'must' reading."

Dr. Robert G. Witty
Founder and President Emeritus, Luther Rice Seminary

"Facts alone make a person smart, but the truth sets a person free! The timing of Dr. Stephen Olford's book entitled, *A Time for Truth*, will undoubtedly catapult the gospel into new arenas of a post-Christian society. In this book, the author masterfully combines faith with fact, principles with practice, and directions with doctrine."

Dr. James O. Davis
National Evangelism Director
Assemblies of God

"Enclosed is a tract for our times—a virtual case study in the futility of knowledge without truth. The only hope for such times is a faithful preacher, who brings God's truth in God's power to bear on human life. It is now, as it was for the 'Preacher,' 'a time for truth.' No one I know can say that to this generation with greater biblical insight, spiritual power, prophetic vision, or personal integrity, than Dr. Stephen Olford."

Dr. Richard Wells
Criswell College

STEPHEN F. OLFORD

a Time for Truth

A STUDY OF ECCLESIASTES 3:1-8

AMG *Publishers*

Chattanooga, TN 37422

A Time for Truth

All Scripture quotations, unless otherwise indicated, are taken from the New King James Version. Copyright ©1982 by Thomas Nelson, Inc. Used by permission. All rights reserved.

Excerpts are taken from:

Shade of His Hand by Oswald Chambers. Copyright © 1924, 1936, 1991 by the Oswald Chambers Publications Assn. Ltd., and used by permission of Discovery House Publishers, Box 3566, Grand Rapids, MI 49501. All rights reserved.

Our Daily Bread, Copyright © 1976 by RBC Ministries, Grand Rapids, MI. Used by permission.

Spirit of the Living God by Daniel Iverson. Copyright © 1963 by Birdwing Music. All rights reserved. Used by permission.

ISBN 0-89957-846-2

Library of Congress Catalog Card Number: 99-64462

Printed in the United States of America
04 03 02 01 00 99 –R– 6 5 4 3 2 1

To Jonathan and David,
"our two sons,"
who have always encouraged me to
"speak the truth in love"
both in
conversation and proclamation

Contents

Foreword

The "father of lies" has successfully infiltrated society with his agenda, and truth is now at a premium. The fact that untruth has become fashionably acceptable is evidenced by the frequent use of qualifiers when one wishes to be taken seriously. "Really!" we exclaim, "This is actually true!" "True truth," "the real truth," "absolutely true. . . ." These are phrases used to distinguish the "actual" from the "fabricated." "When is a politician lying?" we ask. "When his mouth is open!" is the cynic's rejoinder. And here is the most telling question of all . . . a question which reveals the effectiveness of the enemy's agenda: "Preacher! Is that really true or are you just preaching?"

Against this backdrop of dark deceit, my friend, Stephen Olford, has said, "Enough is enough! This is **a time for truth!**" And his most recent book, bearing that same title, is raised as a bright torch against the darkness.

Freedom is a factor of one's environment. A fish, for instance, is not free in the upper atmosphere but in the depths of the ocean. Similarly, a bird is not free in those same depths but when winging through the sky. But in what kind of environment is the Christian truly free?

The proper environment for believers, the one in which we can experience genuine freedom, is none other than the

Word of God. Our Lord said, "If you abide in My word, you are My disciples indeed. And you shall know the truth, and the truth shall make you free" (John 8:31–32). When our behavior is directed by and consistent with the Word of God we walk in freedom. The moment we choose our path on the basis of worldly information we become enslaved to the world.

The "Preacher" of Ecclesiastes discovered this principle "the hard way." In a relentless search for freedom and fulfillment, he drank deeply from the cups of this world's wisdom only to discover that each left the bitter aftertaste of disillusionment and disappointment. Today, this "preacher" can help save us from the same experience by sharing his testimony and its powerful conclusion in a twelve-chapter sermon bearing the same name. Stephen Olford has, in his usual and thorough fashion, found and crystallized the truths of part of that message and now opens them for our benefit.

We are indebted both to the "Preacher" of Ecclesiastes and to our twentieth century preacher and author for this remarkable book. It is, indeed, **a time for truth!**

Dr. Thomas D. Elliff
First Southern Baptist Church
Del City, Oklahoma

Acknowledgements

The chapters in this book are the finished product of messages delivered extemporaneously to audiences around the world and in the churches I have served. In the "flow" of such preaching, many quotes, concepts, and illustrations were brought to mind without specific documentation. I, therefore, acknowledge all sources of such material—heard or read—from the "gifts of men" (Eph. 4:8) with which our risen Lord has enriched the church.

I also acknowledge with gratitude the faithful and efficient efforts of Jennifer Balmer, my projects assistant, in typing and preparing this manuscript.

Then I must thank my dear friend and colleague Dr. Tom Elliff, senior pastor of First Southern Baptist Church in Del City, Oklahoma, and former president of the Southern Baptist Convention, for writing the foreword to this book. As always, in his many writings, he is clear, creative, and convincing. Thank you, dear brother!

Stephen F. Olford

Preface

*D*r. W. Stanford Reid, in his article entitled "Jesus Christ: Focal Point of Knowledge," says:

> In this final third of the twentieth century man faces chaos in knowledge. Acquisition of information has accelerated at such a rate over the past two decades that man has not yet caught up with and assimilated all he has discovered. Even computers have not enabled him to break the log-jam. Perhaps he will eventually 'catch up with himself,' but even if he does, he will still be unable to integrate his thinking unless his whole outlook changes radically. (1968, 3)

> In 1971 a typical state-of-the-art computer processor handled 40,000 instructions per second. Today's state-of-the-art computer handles 40 million instructions per second. Our challenge is to extract knowledge from information and bring about change. Information is power only if it can be used for action. Communication is dynamic and causes action. Computers and telecommunications technologies are converging to process information and communicate that information in order to create positive change. (Johnson 1995, 40)

Computers can figure out all kinds of problems, except the things in this world that just don't add up.

The fact of the matter is that a gullible public is being brainwashed with information without revelation. Such dissemination of "knowledge" very often transmits more error than truth. This is a frightening state of affairs in the world of communication, and certainly anticipates the day when men and women will refuse to "love the truth" and will "believe the lie" (2 Thess. 2:10, 11, NIV). Needless to say, it is Satan himself who is behind all this godless propaganda, for it is he who "deceives the whole world" (Rev. 12:9, NASB). And I believe that in the light of all that is being said and done to capture the minds of young and old today, it is **a time for truth.**

To illustrate this **time for truth**, I have selected a piece of poetry which comprehends and yet compresses most of life into eight verses—from birth to death and war to peace. To each of these life-time experiences, God has a word of truth to say (see Introduction). This means that as we live our lives here on earth, we are not obliged to look to the world system around us for direction or demands regarding how or why we should behave. We have an inerrant body of truth for "all matter of faith and practice" in the Word of God. The Bible may have been banned from our schools, our homes, and even some of our pulpits today, but, thank God, **not** from its availability to any one who wants to know the truth. We are not to fall prey to the scourge of post-modernism, which denies absolute truth for the subjective and inductive method of "your opinion is no better than my opinion, so let's agree to differ since there's no absolute truth!" God has forever given us His plumb line of truth by which all of life is to be measured. Our task is to rightly divide the Word of Truth (see 2 Tim. 2:15) and then obey it with thanksgiving in our hearts! Ultimately, the inscribed truth which we read in the Holy Bible is the incarnate truth which we see in the holy One who said, "I am . . . the truth" (John 14:6).

In the words of Dr. Reid:

> This means that Christ becomes to the Christian the integrating principle of all knowledge because He created, sustains, and redeems both the knower and the object of his knowledge (Rom. 8:23 ff.). The redeemed man now sees light in Christ's light. True, he does not claim to know how all things are related to one another and to the divine central point. But he does believe that all knowledge is so bound together that it is part of one great system, founded, not upon some abstract logical or mathematical principle, but upon the person of the living, risen Lord, who by His Spirit leads His people into all truth. (1968)

As this book goes forth on its mission, it is my earnest prayer that God, by His Holy Spirit, will be pleased to authenticate the truth, as it is in Christ, to all who peruse its pages.

Stephen F. Olford

Introduction

*I*n a day of rabid relativism, it is high **time for truth!**
Relativism is the pervasively held view that ethical
truths depend upon the individuals or groups that
hold them. There is no absolute truth or plumb line by which
to measure up to what a holy God demands of His creatures.
This philosophy of life has brought us to the moral declension
we see in every part of the so-called civilized world.

The tragedy is that relativism has also invaded the church
of Christ. Failure to preach God's inerrant word, in the power
of the Holy Spirit, has led to what Dr. A. W. Tozer (1991)
called "golden-calf Christianity." He writes:

> It is scarcely possible in most places to get anyone to
> attend a meeting where the only attraction is God!
>
> So we have the strange anomaly of orthodoxy in
> creed and heterodoxy in practice. The striped-candy
> technique has been so fully integrated into our present
> religious thinking that it is simply taken for granted. Its
> victims never dream that it is not a part of the teachings
> of Christ and His apostles.
>
> Any objection to the carryings on of our present
> golden-calf Christianity is met with the triumphant

reply: "But we are winning them!" And winning them to what? To true discipleship? To cross-carrying? To self-denial? To separation from the world? To crucifixion of the flesh? To holy living? To nobility of character? To a despising of the world's treasures? To hard self-discipline? To love for God? To total committal to Christ?

Of course, the answer to all these questions is NO! We are paying a frightful price for our religious boredom. And that at the expense of the world's mortal peril!

It is **a time for truth;** and to expound what is meant by this, I have chosen a passage of Scripture which compresses God's sovereign disposition and arrangement of every detail of a person's life into a poem (Eccl. 3:1–8). There is not an experience in this time-frame of life for which there is not a corresponding word of God's truth. This will become obvious as we work our way through this poem in its antithetical form. In the Hebrew text, passages like this are arranged in parallel columns, so that one "time" always stands under another. A similar arrangement is found in Joshua 12:9, containing a catalogue of the conquered Canaanite kings, and in Esther 9:7–9, giving the names of Haman's ten sons. In this present passage we have fourteen pairs of contrast, ranging from external circumstances to the inner affections of a being. This form of presentation was designed under the providence of God to make the truth meaningful and memorable. I remember that after I preached these messages at Calvary Baptist Church in New York City, one young lady cross-stitched the entire passage and framed it for me. The rest of the congregation memorized it!

Ecclesiastes is not an easy book to expound. It is said that Martin Luther doubted whether any exposition up to his time had fully mastered it! But this is part of the divine canon of Scripture, and it behooves us to "rightly divide it as the Word of Truth."

My treatment of it is very simple. I take each couplet of the poem and expound its natural meaning in the light of its spiritual message, using the rest of Scripture for personal application.

The underlying message of this poem is that God has appointed fixed laws for the well-being of His people (Eccl. 3:1–8), having given every human being a consciousness of another life (3:11). He has made it clear that man's wisdom and happiness depend entirely on obedience to His Word (3:12–13) and in the full assurance of His faithfulness and our accountability (3:14–15).

So it is **a time for truth.**

> To every thing there is a season,
> A time for every purpose under heaven:
> A time to be born, And a time to die;
> A time to plant, And a time to pluck what is planted;
> A time to kill, And a time to heal;
> A time to break down, And a time to build up;
> A time to weep, And a time to laugh;
> A time to mourn, And a time to dance;
> A time to cast away stones, And a time to gather stones;
> A time to embrace, And a time to refrain from embracing;
> A time to gain, And a time to lose;
> A time to keep, And a time to throw away;
> A time to tear, And a time to sew;
> A time to keep silence, And a time to speak;
> A time to love, And a time to hate;
> A time of war, And a time of peace.

Ecclesiastes 3:1–8

A Time for Every Purpose Under Heaven

*H*istory records that the noted botanist, Linnaeus, once devised a clock of flowers. Each of the blooms opened in turn at a set time of day. God has a similar order and beauty in the garden of life. Carefully, steadily, He unfolds the petals of time before us so that we may extract from them the nectar of His mercy and the honey of His neverfailing blessings (Bosch 1976).

It is this orderliness of creation which inspired the Preacher to affirm, "To everything there is a season, a time for every purpose under heaven" (3:1). Quite obviously, it is God—and God alone—who winds up the clock of the universe and manages its intricate machinery. This is the only answer which satisfies the Bible, history, and personal experience. He alone regulates time, and He alone relegates time. If, therefore, we would understand the meaning of destiny we must examine these two propositions.

It Is God Who Regulates Time

While time is a human concept, since God is infinite andinhabits eternity, time is nevertheless a gift of His divine agency. Without God there wouldn't be man, and without eternity there wouldn't be time. It follows, therefore, God sovereignly determines that time. Solomon tells us that "[God] has made everything beautiful in its time" (Eccl. 3:11). When it pleased the Creator to determine time, He spoke out of eternity and said, "In the beginning" (Gen. 1:1), and time began. And at some point in the future God will again speak, and time shall be no more. So Solomon adds, "I know that whatever God does, it shall be forever. Nothing can be added to it, and nothing taken from it. God does it, that men should fear before Him" (Eccl. 3:14). Thus we see that man has nothing whatsoever to do with time. Its beginning, duration, and termination are totally outside of his comprehension and control. For this reason time should be regarded by everyone as a precious commodity.

Ted S. Rendall (1964) tells of seeing an hour glass in which the sand was represented by dollar signs. Then he goes on to recall that "after spending an evening too lightly, Robert Murray McCheyne wrote in his diary: 'My heart must break off from all these things. What right have I to steal and abuse my Master's time? The word "redeem," is crying to me.'" The saintly McCheyne had heard the voice of his Master speaking to him from Ephesians 5:15 and 16, "Walk circumspectly, . . . redeeming the time, because the days are evil."

Redeem—that is the key word for the Christian's attitude to *time.* The word gives direction and demands diligence. We are in the market square of life; time is being put up for auction. There are many bidders and we must "redeem" it, buy it for ourselves, in order that we may put it into service for the King.

But beware! You must be awake and alert, or others will put their bid in before you.

Since God sovereignly determines time, we are committed to redeem it for His glory. Let us never have to say, "I wasted time in dreamy unconcern."

But more than this, *time is seasonally divided by God*. The creation story reveals that "God divided the light from the darkness. God called the light Day, and the darkness He called Night. So the evening and the morning were the first day" (Gen. 1:4–5). Later on in the unfolding record of history, we read that God said, "While the earth remains, seedtime and harvest, cold and heat, winter and summer, and day and night shall not cease" (Gen. 8:22). This is the mighty sovereign work of our great God. So we have the daily, nightly, weekly, and yearly seasons, or divisions, of time. In the providence of God, time is thus regulated for our good and for His glory. To reject this doctrine of an overruling God is to fall prey to hopeless atheism and useless nihilism.

Thomas H. Stebbins notes that "Whether our name is Billy Graham or . . . John Doe, each of us receives an equal allotment of 168 hours per week. The difference is in how we spend it. None of us would throw away bits of money—dimes, nickels, pennies—but all of us are guilty of throwing away five minutes here or a quarter of an hour there in our ordinary day." Stebbins (1975) suggests six principles to promote good stewardship of time:

1. Define your goals—both short-range and long.

—In two minutes, write down an all-inclusive list of your lifetime goals—personal, family, career, financial and spiritual.

—In the same length of time, answer the question: "How would I like to spend the next four years?"

—On a third sheet of paper, answer the question: "If I knew I would be struck down by lightning six months from today, how would I live until then?" With proper time management there is no real reason why you should not start doing most of your preferred activities at once.

2. Pursue Your Priorities. It is all too easy to let the urgent crowd out the important, and the important the imperative, until the important and the imperative are postponed or omitted altogether. The only way out is a plan.

[So], divide the next four or five years into one-year segments. List what must be done in each segment in order to accomplish those goals which you believe to be God's will for you. Then get a calendar and work on it a month at a time. . . . A weekly schedule is helpful too.

3. Utilize Your Delays. A University of Wisconsin analysis shows that the average person spends three years of his lifetime just waiting. A Gallup sample of a hundred people selected at random indicated that every one of them expected to do some waiting in the next few hours, yet only one in eight had any plan to utilize the waiting time constructively.

4. Discern God's Timing. We . . . can transform seeming spaces of time into fruitful seasons of harvest: the hour on the plane next to a spiritually needy person, the moments spent waiting for the attendant to refuel our car.

5. Delegate Some Work. Everybody should read the excellent treatment of this principle in *The Master Plan of Evangelism* by Robert E. Coleman (Fleming H. Revell).

6. Take Time Out. In addition to time for quiet meditation and prayer, we need time for rest and recreation. A mature person refuses to become a slave to his work. . . . Even the Puritan pastor Benjamin Colman, back in 1707, when leisure was considered a luxury, wrote, "We daily need some respite and diversion, without which we dull our powers. It spoils the bow to always keep it bent."

But there is a second part to our text:

It Is God Who Relegates Time

The meaning of the words, "a time for every purpose under heaven" (Eccl. 3:1), is all-important to those who want to live for God. What the Preacher is saying is that time is relegated to the fulfillment of God's purpose. Primarily, the word "purpose" or "pleasure" has to do with God's design for the creatures of His hand. And the Bible teaches that God's purpose in relation to this planet is threefold.

There is *the creative purpose of God*. "He has made everything beautiful in its time" (Eccl. 3:11). This was the divine verdict on everything that God created. He saw everything that He had made and "it was very good" (Gen. 1:31). That is why Solomon says, "I know that whatever God does, it shall be forever. Nothing can be added to it, and nothing taken from it. God does it, that men should fear before Him" (Eccl. 3:14). Into that paradise of beauty, however, Satan came and spoiled it all. The plain fact is that "through one man sin entered the world, and death through sin, and thus death spread to all men, because all sinned" (Rom. 5:12). Heaven's answer to this marring of God's creative purpose was immediate and redemptive.

Following the fall of man, therefore, there was introduced the *redemptive purpose of God*. We read that "He . . . put eternity in [men's] hearts, except that no one can find out the work that God does from beginning to end" (Eccl. 3:11). Only the New Testament can interpret these words, for it is the gospel alone that tells us that because of the Savior's work on the cross and His triumphant resurrection, God can put not only eternity, but life and life more abundant into man's heart. (John 10:10). So miraculous is this work of grace that man's unaided mind can never tell how God's Spirit works. This is what Jesus meant when He said: "The wind blows where it wishes, and you hear the sound of it, but cannot tell where it comes from and where it goes. So is everyone who is born of the Spirit" (John 3:8).

If and when this redemptive purpose is rejected by man, then the solemn consequence is *the corrective purpose of God*. "God requires an account of what is past" (Eccl. 3:15), declares the Preacher, and then adds: "Moreover I saw under the sun: In the place of judgment, wickedness was there; and in the place of righteousness, iniquity was there. I said in my heart, 'God shall judge the righteous and the wicked, for there is a time there for every purpose and for every work'" (Eccl. 3:16–17). There is no recourse for those who finally reject the way of salvation. This is the day of grace, and when it is over nothing but judgment awaits the unbelieving and impenitent. This is why the gospel reminds us that "now is the accepted time; behold, now is the day of salvation" (2 Cor. 6:2).

Our text, however, takes us further. Time is not only relegated to the fulfillment of God's purpose, but *time is relegated to the achievement of God's glory*. There is "a time for every purpose under heaven" (Eccl. 3:1). Those two words "under heaven" are not only a reference to this earth, they are also a reminder that everything that happens on this planet is under the eye of God, and therefore, to be done to the glory of God.

Now this is certainly a strange sounding doctrine in the light of the confusion, corruption, and chaos of our modern day! But notwithstanding this, it is still true that God is sovereign, and therefore, will have the last word. God cannot be God and be defeated.

So we learn from Scripture that *God has ordained that the works of man shall praise Him.* The Psalmist observes, "All Your works shall praise You, O Lord, and Your saints shall bless You" (Ps. 145:10). God has so ordered things that everything He has made will ultimately praise Him. This, of course, is especially true of His own people who have become part of the redemptive purpose.

Jesus says to us, "Let your light so shine before men, that they may see your good works and glorify your Father in heaven" (Matt. 5:16). And Paul informs us that "we are His workmanship, created in Christ Jesus for good works, which God prepared beforehand that we should walk in them" (Eph. 2:10). You and I must understand that God has "predestined us. . . , according to the good pleasure of His will, to the *praise* of the glory of His grace" (Eph. 1:5–6). And what goes on in our lives is a constant object lesson to the principalities and powers in heavenly places who observe, in the church, the manifold wisdom of God (see Eph. 3:10).

Truly, God has ordained that the works of man should praise Him.

But more than this, God *has ordained that the wrath of man shall praise Him.* Once again, it is the Psalmist who affirms that "the wrath of man shall praise You" (Ps. 76:10). Indeed, the verse starts with the word "surely"—"*Surely* the wrath of man shall praise You." This is hard to believe, but it is true. God is so wise and strong that He can turn anything to ultimate good and glory.

Think of the life of Joseph (Gen. 30—50). You will recall that he was the favorite son of Jacob, his father, and even before his teen years, God had revealed to him the role that he was to play in the years to come. You will also recall how his brothers rejected the interpretation of his dream; in fact, they became jealous of him, even to the point of attempting to destroy him. At last they sold him to some Egyptians traveling on their way back to their country. To cover their sin they took Joseph's coat of many colors, dipped it in the blood of a slain animal, and presented it to their father with a report that he had been the victim of some wild beast. But God was with Joseph and prospered him until he became the prime minister of Egypt. Then in the providence of God, these same brethren of Joseph had to travel to Egypt to buy food to save their old father and their families in a time of famine. Eventually Joseph revealed himself to his brethren who, in turn, feared lest he should fall upon them and slay them for their cruelty and wickedness. But, instead, he addressed them with these wonderful words: "As for you, you meant evil against me; but God meant it for good, in order to bring it about as it is this day, to save many people alive" (Gen. 50:20). God turned the wrath of man to His eternal praise.

Then reflect on the death of Jesus. No one ever lived such a life of purity, nobility, and humanity. He blessed the little children, He fed the hungry, He healed the sick, He raised the dead, He preached good news to the captives, and yet, at the last, He was nailed to a Roman cross. Watch Him as He carries His wooden burden through the north gate along the Via Dolorosa and up the hill of Calvary. His back is bleeding, His face is bruised, and He staggers due to loss of blood. Presently He arrives at Golgotha, and He is made to lie down upon that gibbet while nails are hammered through His holy hands and feet. The cross is raised and jolted into the ground to dislocate every bone in His body. But looking into the faces of His enemies, He prays, "Father, forgive them, for they do not know what they do" (Luke 23:34). Whatever evil men perpetrated, He turned into good. Indeed, He transformed the very cross on which He died into a throne of grace so that He might mediate eternal redemption to a race of hell-deserving sinners. Through that cross, the wrath of man was turned to His eternal praise. This is why believers can always say, "We know that all things work together for good to those who love God, to those who are the called according to His purpose" (Rom. 8:28).

We can affirm, then, that our God is the God of sovereignty and destiny. He alone can regulate time; He alone can relegate time. To believe in this God is to be delivered from the emptiness and hopelessness of materialism. To believe in this God is to be lifted into the glorious dimensions of divine sovereignty and destiny, and with the hymn writer to sing:

> Immortal, invisible, God only wise,
> In light inaccessible hid from our eyes,
> Most blessed, most glorious, the Ancient of Days,
> Almighty, victorious, Thy great name we praise.
> Walter C. Smith

Think on These Things (Phil. 4:8)

Time is a fragment of eternity given by God to man as a solemn stewardship. The Bible tells us that "we must all appear before the judgment seat of Christ, that each one may receive the things done in the body [life's time-span], according to what he has done, whether good or bad" (2 Cor. 5:10). In the light of this, we need to redeem the time (Eph. 5:16). It was Augustine of Hippo who said, "Time never takes time off."

A Time to Be Born
and A Time to Die

ppointments are part and parcel of our lives! I face appointments every day. I am scheduled for travel appointments, preaching appointments, counseling appointments, eating appointments, and most important of all, my daily appointment with God.

There are, however, two inescapable appointments in the life of every one of us. The one is the hour of our birth, and the other is the hour of our death. Birth ushers us into time, while death ushers us into eternity. God oversees the one and overrules the other. To reject this doctrine is to be a fatalist; to accept it is to be a realist—in the best sense of that word; for the Bible teaches that ultimate reality is to be found in Jesus Christ alone. He claimed, "I am . . . the truth [or reality]. . . . No one comes to the Father except through Me" (John 14:6).

11

From this point on in our study, we have a catalog of contrasts listed in pairs, beginning with the entrance and close of life. The rest of the couplets cover the events and circumstances that take place between these two extremes. In this first contrasting couplet we observe there is "a time to be born, and a time to die" (Eccl. 3:2). The language of the Preacher emphasizes the ordering of a sovereign God, both in our coming into the world and in the way we leave it. There is no question here of untimely births or suicides. In the divinely determined sequence of events, births and deaths have their appointed seasons—without any interference from man. To amplify this a little more fully, let us concentrate, first all, on the fact that:

Birth Is a Sovereign Mystery

We cannot read the Bible or study life without associating the event we call "birth" with the miracle of God—and what a miracle it is! At birth, an heir of immortality is brought into being, because we are "fearfully and wonderfully made" (Ps. 139:14). No wonder Job exclaims: "The Spirit of God has made me, and the breath of the Almighty gives me life!" (Job 33:4). So we see that the whole idea of *mystery* surrounds the miracle of birth. This is true of physical, as well as spiritual, birth. So there is *the mystery of physical birth*. The element of mystery in this whole process of birth is elaborated by Solomon in the 11th chapter of this book and the 5th verse, where he writes, "As you do not know what is the way of the wind, or how the bones grow in the womb of her who is with child, so you do not know the works of God who makes everything." The statement is consistent with medical science. Experts in this field tell us that while there is much we do know about the birth of a child, there is even more that we do not know. For instance, no one has yet been able to decide at what point the fetus becomes "a living being" (Gen. 2:7). And no gynecologist or pediatrician has yet pronounced on the manner in which the bones develop in the womb of a pregnant woman. This entire process, including those parts of the process we think we understand, is shrouded in mystery. With the Psalmist we can sing:

> I will praise You, for I am fearfully and wonderfully made; marvelous are Your works, and that my soul knows very well. My frame was not hidden from You, when *I was made in secret*, and skillfully wrought in the lowest parts of the earth. Your eyes saw my substance, being yet unformed. And in Your book they all were written, the days fashioned for me, when as yet there were none of them (Ps. 139:14–16).

There surely is a divine secret about the event we call physical birth. Have you ever dropped to your knees and looked up into the face of God and said, "O God, thank you for making me just as I am"? You see, God never makes duplicates. He only makes originals. Did you know that you are an original? If you despise your body, your being, then you are despising the work of God. Have you ever said, "Thank you for making me like this. I know there is sin in my life, and I know I have been marred, but I still bear your image, and I still have the potential for all you designed for my life"? Have you ever said, "Thank you"? Say it right now!

There is also *the mystery of spiritual birth*. Speaking to Nicodemus of this, Jesus enounced that "the wind blows where it wishes, and you hear the sound of it, but cannot tell where it comes from and where it goes. So is everyone who is born of the Spirit" (John 3:8). And the apostle John adds that we are born "not of blood, nor of the will of the flesh, nor of the will of man, but of God" (John 1:13). Then there is Peter's statement which reminds us that we are "born again, not of corruptible seed but incorruptible, through the word of God which lives and abides forever" (1 Pet. 1:23).

It appears, therefore, that in that sovereign and mysterious way in which God alone works out His purpose, the Word of God begets faith in Christ, and then the Spirit of God begets life in Christ. We are told for instance that "faith comes by hearing, and hearing by the word of God" (Rom. 10:17). And at the same time, the Spirit of God begets life in Christ, for He is described in Scripture as the Spirit who "gives life" (2 Cor. 3:6). Through the activity of preaching there is the communication of the truth of the Word; and in response to the activity of praying, there is the fertilization of the seed of the Word.

Thus we see that God's supreme agents of spiritual birth are the Word of God and the Spirit of God. The event of birth, whether considered physically or spiritually, is a mystery, and we are dependent upon God for the bringing about of this miracle. Just as God responds to *human* faith when we obey the natural laws of physical birth, so in like manner He responds to saving faith, when we obey the biblical laws of spiritual birth. There is a time to be born physically and a time to be born spiritually; and, just as it necessary to be born into the physical family in order to start our human life, so it is necessary to be born into the spiritual family in order start our divine life.

In his gospel, John tells us that to "as many as received Him, to them He gave the right to become children of God, to those who believe in His name" (John 1:12). Those action words are essential. If we are to know the wonder of spiritual birth, we must believe that the Lord Jesus Christ is the living and saving Word, and then we must receive Him personally and decisively. In response to this act of faith, God effects the new birth, and *life in Christ begins*. What a mystery! What a miracle! Has it happened to you?

So birth is a sovereign mystery; but, by the same token:

Death Is a Solemn Certainty

While birth is shrouded in mystery, death is shrouded with certainty. The fact is that every one will die! While it is impossible to predict with final accuracy the birth of a child, it is possible to say without any reservation that every one of us will eventually die. The only exception to the inevitability of death is the rapture of all living believers at the Second Coming of Christ; otherwise, humanity moves on inexorably to the grave. Throughout Scripture we have such statements as "you shall surely die" (Gen. 2:17); "The soul who sins shall die" (Ezek. 18:4); "The wages of sin is death" (Rom. 6:23); "When desire has conceived, it gives birth to sin; and sin, when it is full-grown, brings forth death" (James 1:15).

This certainty of mortality can mean *the agony of a coming death*. The Bible calls death "the king of terrors" (Job 18:14), and the Psalmist speaks of "the terrors of death" (Ps. 55:4). The writer to the Hebrews expresses the same thought when he describes those "who through fear of death [are] all their lifetime subject to bondage" (Heb. 2:15). This agony, or "anxiety," as the theologians prefer to call it, has three forms. There is the normal anxiety of apprehension before a known cause of danger. For example, a person awaiting serious surgery can be in a state of normal anxiety. Then there is neurotic anxiety, which is a sense of apprehension and fear where there is no definable cause for the anxiety. But, once again, there is the anxiety of life itself, or what has been called the "existential anxiety." Contemporary thinkers are concerned with this third type of anxiety. This anxiety, as Bultmann and others have shown, reveals itself most clearly in the agony of approaching death. This is why all life is spent in postponing death. We breathe, we eat, we exercise, we sleep, we work, we hope, we pray, in order to escape death; indeed, because of this anxiety or agony, latent or expressed, many have committed suicide in order to save themselves from further anxiety. The only cure for such agony is a child-like faith in God and the redemptive use of such anxiety in the winning of other men and women to Jesus Christ. After all, if we know that "it is appointed for men to die once, but after this the judgment" (Heb. 9:27), how diligent, how earnest, how prayerful we ought to be about our loved ones who don't know Jesus Christ. How burdened we should be for our neighbors who are lost, for the millions in the far-flung places of the earth who never have accepted the Savior.

The certainty of mortality can also mean *the tragedy of a Christless death*. The Bible declares, "It is appointed for men to die once, but after this the judgment" (Heb. 9:27). Far greater than the fear of physical death is the fear of spiritual death. The apostle John points this out in his first epistle, where he writes: "Love has been perfected among us in this: that we may have boldness in the day of judgment; because as He is, so are we in this world. There is no fear in love; but perfect love casts out fear, because fear involves torment. But he who fears has not been made perfect in love" (1 John 4:17–18). There is no sadder sight on earth than to watch a dying man or woman approach a Christless eternity.

The tragedy is that, in this day of a revived universalism, men and women are being taught that there is no such place as hell, no such state as "outer darkness," and that all people are redeemed already through the cross of Christ, and therefore, individual salvation is unnecessary. All we have to do is to renew the structures of society in order that we may eliminate the evils of war, poverty, racism, and so on. But this is a humanistic lie which utterly contradicts the clear teaching of the Word of God. Jesus warned, "He who does not believe the Son shall not see life, but the wrath of God abides on him" (John 3:36).

When Pablo Picasso reached his 90th birthday, *Time* magazine celebrated the event by covering his career as an artist. Not mentioned in the *Time* article, but referred to by Harvey Hudson in the Associated Press, was the fact that the famous artist hated birthdays, banned talk of death in his presence, and acted as if he expected to reach 100 (Prairie Bible Institute 1972).

Here was a man who had fame and fortune, and yet nursed a dreaded fear of death. This is so often the combination of factors that mark the world's greatest names. And yet, on the other hand, the humblest believer can know complete deliverance from this fear because the Lord Jesus overcame "him who had the power of death, that is, the devil" (Heb. 2:14). Because of this victory He can *now* deliver "those who through fear of death were all their lifetime subject to bondage" (Heb. 2:15). May God save you from the fact and the fear of a Christless eternity.

It follows, therefore, that for the Christian, the certainty of mortality can *mean the victory of a conquered death*. The apostle Paul cries: "O Death, where is your sting? O Hades, where is your victory? The sting of death is sin, and the strength of sin is the law. But thanks be to God, who gives us the victory through our Lord Jesus Christ" (1 Cor. 15:55–57). Like David, who destroyed Goliath with the giant's own sword, so the greater David has defeated death with death itself. In the language of Isaiah, "He will swallow up death forever" (Is. 25:8). Because of this mighty work of Jesus Christ our Lord, all believers have been saved from spiritual death, and no believer need fear physical death. David knew this experience when he sang: "Though I walk through the valley of the shadow of death, I will fear no evil; for You are with me; Your rod and Your staff, they comfort me" (Ps. 23:4). Later Paul could identify with the Psalmist and confess, "I am hard pressed between the two, having a desire to depart and be with Christ, which is far better" (Phil. 1:23); and again, "To be absent from the body [is] to be present with the Lord" (2 Cor. 5:8). Did you know that death for the Christian is only a tunnel? A dark tunnel for sure, but there is always light on the other side of the tunnel. That is why David said, "Though I walk through the valley of the *shadow* of death" (Ps. 23:4). Where there is a shadow the sun is shining somewhere. And the sun is always shining in Emmanuel's land. For the Christian it is just a release from the limitations and restrictions of this body to be present or "at home" with the Lord, which is a state infinitely better than what we enjoy here. We are enjoying a *good* life here, but it will be a *much better* life then. And when Jesus comes to give us our immortal bodies, we will have the *best* life.

For the genuine Christian, then, the sting, the fear, and the power of death are forever gone. What is more, he can employ the very laws of death to conquer Satan, sin, and self in his everyday experience. Every Christian can overcome Satan by "the blood of the Lamb" (Rev. 12:11). By identification with that same victorious death, every Christian can know victory over sin and self. Indeed, this is the teaching of Romans 6, where we are exhorted to "reckon [ourselves] to be dead indeed to sin, but alive to God in Christ Jesus our Lord [and not to] let sin reign in [our] mortal body, that [we] should obey it in its lusts" (Rom. 6:11–12). And in another place Paul adds, "If [we] live according to the flesh [we] will die; but if by the Spirit [we] put to death the deeds of the body, [we] will live" (Rom. 8:13). Notice the significance of these words. "If [we] live according to the flesh [we] will die." In other words, if we live carnal lives and follow our fleshly nature, we will die. We will die in the sense in which everything we do and say will not have the blessing of God on it. Our prayers will be dead, our devotions will be dead, our Christian life will be dead, and our witness will be dead. Everything we touch will carry corruption. "But if by the Spirit [we] put to death the deeds of the body, [we] will live" (Rom. 8:13). If we count on the Holy Spirit to apply the principle of the cross to our self-life, we will *live*. For the Holy Spirit's ministry is to put to death the deeds of the body, to keep them under subjection in order that the glorious life of the Lord Jesus comes through—that resurrection life, that reigning life, that rejoicing life, that righteous life. This is the glory of the liberated life! As we count upon the Holy Spirit to apply the mortifying power of the cross to our self-life, God be praised! Christ's resurrection life breaks through in victory, power, and blessing. This then, is the victory of a conquered death.

We can choose, then, whether we suffer the agony of a coming death, the tragedy of a Christless death, or enjoy the victory of a conquered death. But just as there is a time to die, in the redemptive sense, there is also a time to be born, in the regenerative sense. In Christ, both death and birth find their ultimate answer! To know Him personally and savingly is to be born again. To know Him personally and savingly is to die to self and sin, and to live eternally unto God. The secret is knowing Jesus Christ as our Lord and Life! That is why He came and looked into the faces of men and women just like you and me and declared, "I have come that [you] may have life, and that [you] may have it more abundantly" (John 10:10). Are you merely existing, or are you really living? Do you know the fullness, wonder, and glory of His life? His whole purpose in coming into this world was that you "may have life, and . . . [life] more abundantly." True, you were born physically, but if you *know* Jesus Christ as your personal Savior, you are born spiritually. Enter into the heritage and glory of His life. Pray and mean:

> Out of my bondage, sorrow, and night,
> Jesus, I come, Jesus, I come;
> Into Thy freedom, gladness, and light,
> Jesus, I come to Thee;
> Out of my sickness into Thy health,
> Out of my want and into Thy wealth,
> Out of my sin and into Thyself,
> Jesus, I come to Thee.
>
> Out of the fear and dread of the tomb,
> Jesus, I come, Jesus, I come;
> Into the joy and light of Thy home,
> Jesus, I come to Thee;
> Out of the depths of ruin untold,

Into the peace of Thy sheltering fold,
Ever Thy glorious face to behold,
Jesus, I come to Thee.

Think on These Things (Phil. 4:8)

We are born again to fulfill God's purpose for our lives. That purpose is "to be conformed to the image of [God's] Son" (Rom. 8:29). We are born again to fulfill God's plan for our lives. That plan "God prepared beforehand that we should walk [in it]" (Eph. 2:10). The road is already built, let's start walking!

3

A Time to Plant
And a Time to Pluck

*I*n a copyrighted editorial in *U.S. News & World Report*
entitled "What Are We Planting?" Marvin Stone
(1977) writes: "It's planting time now for America.
The soil awaits decisions that can either shade and comfort
the future, or create only thickets." The burning questions are:

> Should we go on mindlessly wasting precious natural
> resources, or should we conserve as best we can, keeping
> in mind our children and our children's children? Should
> we perpetuate a welfare system that . . . [fosters] waste and
> corruption? Or should we perform radical surgery to en-
> sure health and wealth for all of us? . . . Should we skimp
> on money for basic research, while spending on bigger
> race tracks and sports palaces, with multimillion-dollar

contracts for young athletes? Or should we also be building better libraries and laboratories, planting the seeds of tomorrow's science and technology? . . . [In a word], what are we planting, anyway?

These are questions we could ask about any nation—and they are necessary and urgent questions—but there are even more important questions facing the church—the church of God's people everywhere.

In the divine order of things, there is a law of harvest that affects every man and woman on earth. It is the law of sowing and reaping. From the age of responsibility to the hour of accountability, we sow and reap. What we sow in youthful days, we reap in older years. What we sow in time, we reap in eternity. So there is "a time to plant, and a time to pluck what is planted" (3:2). The only consolation about this *law* of harvest is that behind it and beyond it is the *Lord* of the harvest. To know Him is to sow and reap to our eternal gain; to ignore Him is to sow and reap to our eternal loss. Let us then address ourselves to this law of harvest:

The Responsibility of Sowing

There is "a time to plant" (Eccl. 3:2). The responsibility of sowing becomes apparent when we apply the four tests of general inquiry.

1. Why should we sow? In the very nature of things, "sowing and reaping" is a law of life. Therefore, to ask, "Why should we sow?" is to challenge the wisdom of God. The apostle Paul exposes the impertinence of questioning Omniscience in this regard when he asks: "O man, who are you to reply against God? Will the thing formed say to him who formed it, 'Why have you made me like this?'" (Rom. 9:20). The fact of the matter is that *all* of life is structured on the law of cause and effect. Thus it happens that when we sow we also reap.

2. What should we sow? One of the world's great thinkers has reminded us:

> Sow a thought, you reap an action;
> Sow an action, you reap a habit:
> Sow a habit, you reap a character:
> Sow a character, you reap a destiny.
>   (Naismith 1962, 193 [1071])

It matters, therefore, what we sow.

In his Epistle to the Galatians, Paul tells us that "he who sows to his flesh will of the flesh reap corruption, but he who sows to the Spirit will of the Spirit reap everlasting life" (Gal. 6:8). The important question then is *what* is "sowing to the Spirit?" To find our answer, we do not need to leave the immediate context. In simple terms, sowing to the Spirit is *loving God* —Galatians 6:7 declares, "God is not mocked; for whatever a man sows, that he will also reap." Loving God is the opposite of mocking God. To *mock* God literally means "to turn up the nose at Him," or "to treat Him with contempt." In the Septuagint, an early Greek translation of the Old Testament, the word is used to describe those who are not prepared to accept that "the fear of the Lord is the beginning of knowledge" (Prov. 1:7). Concerning such, God says, "They would have none of my counsel and *despised* my every rebuke" (Prov. 1:30).

Conversely, the *fear* of God leads to *faith* in God, and faith in God leads, in turn, to the love of God. And it is the office of the Holy Spirit to create in us that love of God through the redemptive merit our Lord Jesus Christ. Only by the Savior's death and resurrection has the groundwork been laid for the sinner's reconciliation to a holy God.

But sowing to the Spirit is not only loving God, it is *loving man*. The apostle exhorts, "As we have opportunity, let us do good to all, especially to those who are of the household of faith" (Gal. 6:10). We are in the world to *sow love*—love to God and love to man. And Paul makes it quite clear that such love is not just sentiment or mere words. According to the apostle, such love is "doing good to all men"; it is meeting human need—spiritually, socially, and economically. John echoes this when he declares:

> By this we know love, because He laid down His life for us. And we also ought to lay down our lives for the brethren. But whoever has this world's goods, and sees his brother in need, and shuts up his heart from him, how does the love of God abide in him? My little children, let us not love in word or in tongue, but in deed and in truth." (1 John 3:16–18)

A great many of the social, moral, and civil problems of our lives today could be solved if we knew how to "sow to the Spirit," for the fruit of the Spirit is love: love to God, and then love to man. So we see that there is a time to plant, and what we should be planting is love.

3. *Where should we sow?* The Master answered this question, once and for all, when He told the parable of the four soils (see Mark 4:1–20).

There is *the dusty soil*. Along the plowed fields were little paths that became hard and dusty with the trampling of feet. The fowls of the air immediately gobbled up seed that fell here. This represents the heart that is defiled by human traffic, and therefore exposed to satanic domination.

There is *the stony soil*. This was ground that had a narrow skim of earth over a shelf of limestone rock. Seed falling on this ground germinated all right, but because of shallowness of earth and lack of moisture, the sprouting seed quickly died. There is such a thing as emotional response to the gospel without theological content and spiritual conviction.

There is *the busy soil*. We are told that the Palestinian farmer was a lazy man in those days. He cut off the top of the weeds, but left the fibrous roots below the surface; consequently, when the new seed began to grow, the old weeds revived in all their strength and choked the harvest. It is possible to be busy for self and lazy for God.Room for pleasure, room for business,

> But for Christ the Crucified,
> Not a place that He can enter,
> In the heart for which He died.
> adapted by Daniel W. Whittle

There is *the ready soil.* This was the good, clean, and deep soil in which the seed always flourished. This is the heart that is ready for the gospel of love in Jesus Christ.

So while it is true that the seed we need to sow is love, it is also true that love will not grow in dusty, stony, or busy soil. Love grows only in ready soil, or good ground.

4. When should we sow? While it is clear that *all* life is sowing and reaping, it is likewise evident that there are two crucial periods in the history of any one of us for sowing and consequent reaping. One is the time of youth, and the other is the time of old age. Ask any farmer, gardener, or forester and he will tell you that the two times for successful planting are spring and autumn. Spring is youth time; autumn is old age.

The emphasis throughout Scripture is on planting when we are young. Solomon says, "Remember *now* your Creator in the days of your youth, before the difficult days come, and the years draw near when you say, 'I have no pleasure in them'" (Eccl. 12:1). There is a springtime of responsiveness. It is the time of comparative innocence, interest, and initiative.

To a lesser degree, the autumn of life is also a time of decision. The failure of life and the fear of death are often the incentives that prompt an older person to seek God and to plant his faith in Jesus Christ. To such, the Bible says, "Behold, now is the accepted time; behold, now is the day of salvation" (2 Cor. 6:2).

So we see there is "a time to plant." But there is also "a time to pluck what is planted," and it involves:

The Accountability of Reaping

With regard for the designed contrast of these couplets, some expositors interpret the plucking up as a reference to the time of judgment and destruction. And without doubt this thought carries validity since we are thinking of the accountability of reaping; but the season of reaping need not always be a time of judgment. It can also be an occasion of joyful harvest. It all depends on how we have sown. Whether in time, or in eternity, reaping has its own inescapable laws.

There is *the law of likeness*. The Bible tells us that "whatever a man sows, that he will also reap" (Gal. 6:7). Then Paul goes on to say, "He who sows to his flesh will of the flesh reap corruption, but he who sows to the Spirit will of the Spirit reap everlasting life" (Gal. 6:8). The apostle does not leave us in doubt as to what that fleshly corruption is. In the previous chapter of the Galatian epistle he writes: "Now the works of the flesh are evident, which are: adultery, fornication, uncleanness, lewdness, idolatry, sorcery, hatred, contentions, jealousies, outbursts of wrath, selfish ambitions, dissensions, heresies, envy, murders, drunkenness, revelries, and the like" (Gal. 5:19–21). And then Paul concludes, "Those who practice such things will not inherit the kingdom of God" (Gal. 5:21). And Jesus confirms this when He warns, "Every plant which My heavenly Father has not planted will be uprooted" (Matt. 15:13). We are accountable for the seed that we have sown and the plants that we have buried in the soil of our past lives, for it is written, "God requires an account of what is past" (Eccl. 3:15).

The story is told of the little boy who, in a moment of spiteful temper, buried his sister's teddy bear. Father, Mother, sister, and even brother looked everywhere for the missing teddy bear, but all in vain. Weeks later, Father was in the garden, doing some weeding, when he called the family to come quickly and see a strange sight. With the family around him, he pointed to a piece of ground where fresh blades of grass appeared in the pattern of a teddy bear! What the small boy had not realized was that the buried teddy bear was stuffed with a cheap grade of grass seed! How true are those biblical words, "Be sure your sin will find you out" (Num. 32:23).

Thank God, however, that "he who sows to the Spirit will of the Spirit reap everlasting life" (Gal. 6:8). And the apostle tells us that "the fruit of the Spirit is love, joy, peace, longsuffering, kindness, goodness, faithfulness, gentleness, self-control. Against such there is no law" (Gal. 5:22–23). This is the harvest that will receive our Lord's "well done" and will endure throughout eternity. To pluck this fruit and present it to Christ in glory should be the supreme ambition of every Christian.

What kind of harvest are we expecting in that day? We must realize that sowing and reaping have a law of likeness. If we have sown to the flesh, we will reap of the flesh corruption; on the other hand, if we have sown to the Spirit, we will reap of the Spirit life everlasting.

But reaping has another law: it is *the law of increase*. When Jesus told of the seed that fell on the good ground, He said that it brought forth some thirtyfold, some sixtyfold, and some a hundredfold (Matt. 13:8). Now this is true of all reaping. Not only do we harvest *likeness in kind* but also *increase of kind*. This must be a terrifying thought to those who sow to the flesh! Think of the multiplied corruption that awaits judgment day! But for the Spirit-filled Christian, it is not only going to be fruit or more fruit, but *much fruit*. Jesus said, "By this My Father is glorified, that you bear *much fruit*; so you will be My disciples" (John 15:8).

Let me ask you if this law of likeness is matched by the law of increase in your life? As you grow day by day in the Lord Jesus, are people seeing more love, more joy, more peace, more longsuffering, more kindness, more goodness, more faithfulness, more gentleness, more self-control? Is the Holy Spirit reproducing in you the likeness of the Lord Jesus? Can people say that you remind them of Jesus? This is what Christian living is all about. Has it ever occurred to you that God's purpose in redemption is to populate heaven with men and women who are like His dear Son, and in the meantime, to populate earth with men and women who are like His dear Son—conformed to His image. This is the supreme ambition of my heart. With Robert Murray McCheyne I say every day, "Oh God, make me as holy as a saved sinner can be." In the words of our text, my desire is that as I plant day by day the seeds of prayer, Bible study, and yieldedness to the Holy Spirit, the life of the Lord Jesus is going to be manifested in me.

The lesson of our text is plain. We are responsible for our sowing, and we are also accountable for our reaping. What kind of harvests are we expecting? God's purpose for our lives is likeness to the Lord Jesus! How are you planting? What are you planting? When are you planting? Are you busy at this planting business? Once again I must remind you, "Whatever a man sows, that he will also reap" (Gal. 6:7). Harvest day is coming. One day you will have to stand before that judgment seat of Christ, and the harvest you have reaped will be evaluated (2 Cor. 5:10). What kind of harvest are you expecting? Is it likeness to the Lord Jesus? This involves sowing the seeds of daily prayer. Have you a personal altar; have you a family altar where you kneel to pray with your loved ones? Are you sowing the seeds of regular Bible reading. Do you read the Word of God every day? The only way that we can be like Jesus is by looking into the mirror of His Word and having the Holy Spirit mold us into the image of Jesus that we see in the Word—from one degree of glory to another. Our daily prayer should be:

> Earthly pleasures vainly call me,
> I would be like Jesus;
> Nothing worldly shall enthrall me,
> I would be like Jesus.

Be like Jesus, this my song,
In the home and in the throng;
Be like Jesus, all day long!
I would be like Jesus.

Rowe

Think on These Things (Phil. 4:8)

"Sowing and reaping" is an immutable law of God. This is true especially in Christian living. The great hindrances to such good living are weariness and discouragement. Four months elapse between planting and harvest (John 4:35), and while it is true that in spiritual sowing the results occasionally come sooner, it is also true that more often the results take longer. So Paul warns us with two imperatives: "[Do] not grow weary" and "do not lose heart" (Gal. 6:9). The apostle emphasizes this when he affirms that "the *hard-working* farmer must be *first* to partake of the crops" (2 Tim. 2:6).

A Time to Kill
And a Time to Heal

We live in a world of cruelty, violence, and death. At times we wonder whether there is any overruling power behind the chaos and confusion we see around us; and yet the Bible says there is "a time to kill, and a time to heal" (Eccl. 3:3). Quite obviously, it is God alone who can give life, and it is God alone who can take life. In each case, God claims this prerogative. He declares, "I kill and I make alive; I wound and I heal" (Deut. 32:39). How this can be interpreted and understood in the framework of human experience constitutes one of the great themes of biblical revelation.

"A time to kill, and a time to heal" (Eccl. 3:3) are startling words indeed, and for this reason people throughout the centuries have interpreted them in various ways. Some scholars have thought that they refer to war. Others have limited the meaning to surgical operations performed with a view to saving life. Still others have maintained that the text is speaking of the execution of criminals and the defense of the oppressed. Before we jump to conclusions, however, let's give attention to:

The Problem of Killing

It must be pointed out from the very start that killing is a direct result of sin. Until our first parents bowed to the enticements of sin there was no such experience as death; but then sin came into the world "and death through sin, and thus death spread to all men, because all sinned" (Rom. 5:12). Notwithstanding the fact that killing results from sin, however, the taking of life can never happen without the knowledge and permission of a sovereign God. Thus the Bible teaches us that there is killing within *the permissive will of God*, and that there are two main forms of killing in this category.

There is, first of all, *suicide*, which is the murder of one's self. Concerning suicide, God insists, "You shall not murder" (Ex. 20:13). There have been infidels in all ages who have advocated self-murder as a justified means of release from trial and difficulty, but thinking men as far back as Aristotle have generally considered it as cowardly and unreasonable under any circumstance. No man has the right to take his own life, any more than the life of another. The Word of God makes plain that the length of days is one of the tokens of divine blessing, and it is interesting that the Scriptures do not mention one single instance of a good man who committed suicide. Normally, suicide is not the act of a moment; it is the climax to a process. Men and women commit suicide when they resign themselves to the inexorable law of sin. The Bible says, "The wages of sin is death" (Rom. 6:23); and again, "When desire has conceived, it gives birth to sin; and sin, when it is full-grown, brings forth death" (James 1:15). Suicide merely hastens the outworking of this law within the permissive will of God.

Then there is *homicide*, which is the murder of one's fellow man. Once again, God commands, "You shall not murder" (Ex. 20:13). To violate this divine commandment is to commit murder. Needless to say, there is more than one way of killing our fellow man, and it does not always necessitate the lowering of ourselves to the methods and motives of a gangster or terrorist. But as in the case of suicide, homicide is but the accelerated outworking of the law of sin. It is true that in homicide innocent people are often involved, but it must be recognized that after death comes the day of judgment, when the real culprits will have to answer before a holy God.

The Bible also teaches us that there is killing within *the directive will of God*. A study of Scripture seems to indicate that in the sovereignty of God there is directive killing for two purposes.

The first is what we might term the *consumptive* purpose. Under the Mosaic system, innumerable birds and beasts were slain every year for the sacrifices. So it seems plain from the Holy Scriptures that it was legal to eat the flesh of animals, of birds, and of fish. Indeed, even Christ Himself ate of the Passover lamb and partook of broiled fish (Luke 22:15; 24:42).

The second has to do with the *corrective* purpose of killing. The sixth commandment does not prohibit lawful killing in the case of self defense (personally or nationally), nor does it prohibit capital punishment (of an individual or a nation). Even before the giving of the law God declared: "Whoever sheds man's blood, by man his blood shall be shed; for in the image of God He made man" (Gen. 9:6). From these stern words we are obliged to acknowledge that there is a place in God's directive will for capital punishment. So it is written, "He who strikes a man so that he dies shall surely be put to death" (Ex. 21:12). History, both sacred and profane, makes it perfectly clear that the Almighty has used nations to work out His own corrective purpose. Isaiah refers to the Assyrians as "the rod of My anger"

(Is. 10:5), and Habakkuk indicates that the Chaldeans were raised up as instruments of judgment (Hab. 1:6). It appears, therefore, that there are times when war is sovereignly directed to punish evil on a national or international scale. The fact that innocent people are killed in the process only serves to magnify the sacrifice that is involved in dealing with the exceeding sinfulness of sin.

For those who think that directive killing is only an Old Testament concept, there is that 13th chapter of Romans, where we read: "There is no authority except from God. . . . Therefore whoever resists the authority resists the ordinance of God, and those who resist will bring judgment on themselves. For rulers are not a terror to good works, but to evil" (Rom. 13:1–3). To make his point, the apostle Paul adds: "Do what is good, and you will have praise from the same. For he is God's minister to you for good. But if you do evil, be afraid; for he does not bear *the sword* in vain; for he is God's minister, an avenger to execute wrath on him who practices evil. Therefore you must be subject, not only because of wrath but also for conscience' sake" (Rom. 13:3–5).

Then there is killing within *the redemptive will of God*. The supreme example of this is the precious death of our Lord and Savior, Jesus Christ. Because of your sin and mine it was necessary that One should die in the place of many, if the human race were to be redeemed. So Jesus willingly exposed Himself to the stroke of divine judgment against sin. The Bible tells us "Christ also suffered once for sins, the just for the unjust, that He might bring us to God, *being put to death in the flesh* but made alive by the Spirit" (1 Pet. 3:18). Because of that death you and I can live eternally.

The principle of redemptive killing can also be applied to our own self-life in order that we might live entirely unto God. "If [we] live according to the flesh [we] will die; but if by the Spirit [we] put to death the deeds of the body, [we] will live" (Rom. 8:13).

There is a time to kill, and whether that moment of destiny falls within the permissive, directive, or redemptive will of God is not ours to question. Your responsibility and mine is to bow to the sovereign will of Deity and to exclaim with Job, "The Lord gave, and the Lord has taken away; Blessed be the name of the Lord" (Job 1:21). Until we accept God's will in this regard, the problem of killing will always be a problem. And while on this side of heaven we shall never be able to understand everything, it is possible to have a faith in the ultimate overruling of God in the affairs of men, even in the presence of killing.

But now let us turn to the other aspect of our subject:

The Promise of Healing

There is no passage which speaks to this ministry of healing more eloquently than the closing verses of James (5:13–20). To study this passage is to discover that there are five aspects of this promise of healing.

1. The Promise of Emotional Healing. "Is anyone among you suffering? Let him pray. Is anyone cheerful? Let him sing psalms" (James 5:13). The emotional life of a Christian community is tremendously important. God intends that we should live emotionally balanced lives that are unaffected by the extremes of unrealistic optimism, on the one hand, or unbearable pessimism on the other. Our individual joys or sorrows can affect the life of the whole community. James teaches that if there is an affliction or a sorrow in the life of the church, it should be brought to God in the fellowship of prayer. If there is merriment, or more literally, "the enjoyment of soul health," this, too, should be shared in prayer. So whether it is praying or praising, both are part of the life of the church.

Thus the answer to the emotional problem is *fellowship in prayer*. I use the word "fellowship" deliberately, for we, as members of the church, are not isolated entities. No one can say, "I am not wanted," or "I do not matter." We are an integral part of the church, and if God is going to use us as a corporate Body, the first lesson we must learn is that of fellowship in prayer. As we share our sorrows and joys in the communion of prayer, the emotional problems will be solved and the church will know an emotionally balanced life.

So we are to "bear one another's burdens, and so fulfil the law of Christ" (Gal. 6:2); and again, to "rejoice with those who rejoice, and weep with those who weep" (Rom. 12:15). Here, then, is the secret of emotional healing.

2. The Promise of Physical Healing. "Is anyone among you sick? Let him call for the elders of the church, and let them pray over him, anointing him with oil in the name of the Lord. And the prayer of faith will save the sick, and the Lord will raise him up. And if he has committed sins, he will be forgiven" (James 5:14–15). It is quite clear from these verses that the purpose of God is that the church should enjoy relatively good physical health. If there is continual sickness, it can be indicative of something radically wrong. Suffering and sickness are ultimately caused by Satan and sin.

Paul, who had "a thorn in the flesh" attributed it to the devil. He called it "a messenger of Satan to buffet me" (2 Cor. 12:7). It is true that this was allowed by the Lord in order that through the weakness of his body the power of Christ might rest upon him. Other sicknesses, however, are caused directly by sin, as is evidenced by the physical condition of certain believers in the Corinthian church. Having referred to their unworthy conduct, Paul adds, "For this reason many are weak and sick among you, and many sleep" (1 Cor. 11:30).

Sometimes the Lord allows sickness to prove and perfect His people, as in the case of Job. Addressing the devil, He said, "Have you considered My servant Job, that there is none like him on the earth" (Job 1:8). And it will be remembered that through the process of suffering Job was proved and perfected.

Other times, the Lord allows suffering in order to punish and purify. Concerning the immoral person who was found in the Corinthian church, Paul had to urge the members to "deliver such a one to Satan for the destruction of the flesh, that his spirit may be saved in the day of the Lord Jesus" (1 Cor. 5:5). And then we are familiar with those words in Hebrews 12, verses 6 and 10: "For whom the LORD loves He chastens, and scourges every son whom He receives. . . . For they indeed for a few days chastened us as seemed best to them, but He for our profit, that we may be partakers of His holiness."

Bearing all this in mind, it is quite clear from the passage before us that God intends that healing for His people should come through *faithfulness in prayer*. The words are clear, "And the prayer of faith will save the sick, and the Lord will raise him up" (James 5:15). The faithfulness in prayer must be accompanied by the anointing with oil (which is symbolic of the Holy Spirit's part in healing, Rom. 8:11), the praying of the elders, and the confessing of every known sin. And in response to such faithfulness in praying, God promises divine healing within the bounds of His permissive will. Sometimes His permissive will is death itself which ushers the believer into the realm of perfect health and peace. To be with Christ is "far better" (Phil. 1:23).

3. The Promise of Personal Healing. "Confess your trespasses to one another, and pray for one another, that you may be healed" (James 5:16). The healing mentioned here is not necessarily physical. It is more likely the healing of disharmonies and divisions in the life of the church, a healing of relationships. God's purpose for every local church is that it may enjoy "the unity of the Spirit in the bond of peace" (Eph. 4:3). Such harmony is described by the Psalmist as "good" and "pleasant" (Ps. 133:1).

So James maintains that when there is disunity in the church there must be *forgiveness in prayer*. This same truth was enunciated by the Lord when He said: "If you bring your gift to the altar, and there remember that your brother has something against you, leave your gift there before the altar, and go your way. First be reconciled to your brother, and then come and offer your gift" (Matt. 5:23–24). In response to such forgivingness in prayer there can be personal healing.

4. *The Promise of National Healing*. Elijah "prayed earnestly that it would not rain; and it did not rain on the land for three years and six months. And he prayed again, and the heaven gave rain, and the earth produced its fruit" (James 5:17–18). James brings the prayer life of Elijah into this context to illustrate how "the effective, fervent prayer of a righteous man avails much" (v. 16). God had scourged His backsliding people with a drought. In answer to the prayer of a simple man—for he "was a man with a nature like ours" (v. 17)—we read that "the heaven gave rain, and the earth produced its fruit" (v. 18).

National healing can come to a country when men and women like Elijah know *fervency in prayer*. It is "the effective, *fervent* prayer of a righteous man [which] avails much" (James 5:16). God emphasizes the same truth when He says, "If My people who are called by My name will humble themselves, and pray and seek My face, and turn from their wicked ways, then I will hear from heaven, and will forgive their sin and heal their land" (2 Chr. 7:14).

5. *The Promise of Spiritual Healing*. "Brethren, if anyone among you wanders from the truth, and someone turns him back, let him know that he who turns a sinner from the error of his way will save a soul from death and cover a multitude of sins" (James 5:19–20). Although prayer is not specifically mentioned in these two verses, it is quite obvious that James intends this spiritual healing to be linked with the power of prayer. The secret here is *friendliness in prayer*. Only such loving friendship will restore the erring brother or convert the straying sinner. As we pray for the erring *brother*, let us ever remember Paul's words, "Brethren, if a man is overtaken in any trespass, you who are spiritual restore such a one in a spirit of gentleness, considering yourself lest you also be tempted" (Gal. 6:1). The required discernment, meekness, and tenderness for this spiritual healing comes only through the power of prayer. Then as we pray for the *straying sinner*, let us recall that the Lord Jesus said, "If a man has a hundred sheep, and one of them goes astray, does he not leave the ninety-nine and go to the mountains to seek the one that is straying?" (Matt. 18:12). No wonder the Good Shepherd was called "a friend of . . . sinners" (Matt. 11:19). He was ever after the lost sheep.

Spiritual healing can be effected only through a friendship which is willing to plead and bleed for those who have strayed. So Isaiah reminds us, "All we like sheep have gone astray; we have turned, every one, to his own way" (Is. 53:6). But with that fact there is the other truth, "He was wounded for our transgressions, He was bruised for our iniquities; the chastisement for our peace was upon Him, and by His stripes we are healed" (Is. 53:5).

So we have examined the problem of killing and our hearts have been solemnized; but thank God, there is the promise of healing for problems that are emotional, physical, personal, national, and spiritual. We are living in a broken world, a bruised world. Talk to anyone on the street, in a taxi cab, or in an airplane and you will discover the hurt, the harm, the hopelessness in human lives. The Bible says, "If one member suffers, all the members suffer" (1 Cor. 12:26). Of course, this is true of the church of Jesus Christ; but in a sense, it is true of this whole creation. Scripture informs us that "the whole creation groans and labors with birth pangs together until now" (Rom. 8:22). And then Paul adds, "Not only that, but *we also* who have the firstfruits of the Spirit, even we ourselves groan within ourselves" (Rom. 8:23). Why? Because we are linked to a groaning creation. God in heaven feels it, and if we are indwelt by the Holy Spirit, then we ought to feel it. But thank

God, with all the hurt there is healing. And through the "wounding" and "bruising" of our blessed Savior we can know holiness, and we can minister healing. With Peter we can reflect on the One who "bore our sins in His own body on the tree, that we, having died to sins, might live for righteousness—by whose stripes [we are] healed" (1 Pet. 2:24).

Think on These Things (Phil. 4:8)

The subject of this chapter vividly brings to mind the massacre in Littleton, Colorado. There was *the killing.* Two male teenagers who were rootless, restless, ruthless, and, alas, remorseless, murdered twelve of their peers and a beloved teacher and coach. This is what the human heart, without Christ and the moral constraints of God's laws, is capable of perpetrating. God help us! But there was also *the healing* (still on-going). Who did people turn to? The Church, of course! When Larry King interviewed the parents of Cassie Bernall, who was cut down by a bullet to her head—even as she was testifying to her faith in God—Mr. and Mrs. Bernall, like Jesus on the cross, spoke healing words of forgiveness. The peace they modeled was truly remarkable! There is a healing joy that comes when we decide to "forgive those who trespass against us."

A Time to Break Down
And a Time to Build Up

For fourteen years it was my privilege to pastor the Calvary Baptist Church of New York City. During that period my wife and I literally lived on the job, and from the lofty windows of the hotel suite we called home we monitored quite a panorama of happenings in that great "Fun City." One common sight that lingers in my memory is that of busy workmen, falling debris, loaded trucks, to be followed later by eager builders, giant cranes, and rising buildings. The more I reflected upon this "daily happening" in the life of a city, the more I saw a spiritual principle in the architectural formula of demolishing the old before establishing the new.

The work of grace in the human soul may be divided into two distinct operations of the Holy Spirit. The first is to break

41

down rebellious lives into nothingness and self-abasement before God, and the other is to exalt the crucified and risen Jesus as Lord upon the ruins of repentant lives that are open to the grace of God.

With this as our clue, let us look at:

The Challenge of God to Demolish the Old Building

In the symbolism of Scripture, the human life is often spoken of as a building. For instance, our Lord Jesus said, "Whoever hears these sayings of Mine, and does them, I will liken him to a wise man who built his house on the rock" (Matt. 7:24). The house He was referring to was the entire structure of the human life.

Now apart from God no man can build a house that will endure for eternity. In fact, because "all have sinned and fall short of the glory of God" (Rom. 3:23), every human building has been condemned. In spite of this condemnation, however, people still persist in living their lives apart from God; God does not get through to them. It follows, therefore that before a new building can be established, the old one must be demolished, and the only way to accomplish this is to knock down the walls. Significantly enough, when the four walls are demolished, the roof that shuts us off from God inevitably collapses!

Let us then consider the four walls that have to be demolished before we can start building anew. In man's response to God's call of salvation, there are four biblical conditions that are clearly laid down. The first is repentance, the second is faith, the third is obedience, and the fourth is forgiveness. The walls that shut us off from God are the opposite of these conditions. Let us take them one by one.

1. The wall of unbrokenness must be demolished. In the ministry of John the Baptist, then later of our Lord, and finally of the apostles, the note of *repentance* was always sounded as a prerequisite for entrance into the kingdom of God. Paul sums this up when he testifies "to Jews, and also to Greeks, repentance toward God and faith toward our Lord Jesus Christ" (Acts 20:21). Repentance means a change of mind leading to a change of life. It implies and involves a true spirit of brokenness.

Naaman the leper illustrates how the spirit of unbrokenness can change to true repentance (see 2 Kgs. 5:1–27). It will be remembered that he came to the prophet Elisha, requesting that the man of God might "heal him of his leprosy" (2 Kgs. 5:6). The prophet told him to wash in the Jordan River seven times and promised that, as a result, his leprosy would be cleansed. On hearing these instructions we read in 2 Kgs. 5:11–12 that:

> Naaman became furious, and went away and said, "Indeed, I said to myself, 'He will surely come out to me, and stand and call on the name of the Lord his God, and wave his hand over the place, and heal the leprosy.' Are not the Abanah and the Pharpar, the rivers of Damascus, better than all the waters of Israel? Could I not wash in them and be clean?" So he turned and went away in a rage.

Here is graphically dramatized the spirit of unbrokenness. But Naaman had discerning servants, and they came to him and pleaded that he would change his mind and reconsider his ways; and amazingly enough, for a man as proud as Naaman, he did repent, and he went down to the Jordan and dipped himself seven times. That activity of dipping symbolizes true repentance and brokenness; and as a result, we read that "his flesh was restored like the flesh of a little child, and he was clean" (2 Kgs. 5:14). Here, then, is one wall that must be demolished, if our lives are to be built anew.

2. *The wall of unbelief must be demolished.* The Bible specifically states, "Without faith it is impossible to please

Him, for he who comes to God must believe that He is, and that He is a rewarder of those who diligently seek Him" (Heb. 11:6). Indeed, the Word of God declares, "Whatever is not from faith is sin" (Rom. 14:23). Just as God cannot get through to us without brokenness and repentance, so it is equally true that He cannot do anything for us without faith.

Even though an apostle, Thomas was a man who disbelieved. He could say in the presence of those who had actually seen the risen Lord, "Unless I see in His hands the print of the nails, and put my finger into the print of the nails, and put my hand into His side, *I will not believe*" (John 20:25). In grace and mercy Jesus later confronted unbelieving Thomas and said, "Do not be unbelieving, but believing" (John 20:27). Hearing those words Thomas was thoroughly convicted of his sin of unbelief and cried, "My Lord and my God!" (John 20:28).

If we want God to do anything for us, we must "believe that He is, and that He is a rewarder of those who diligently seek Him" (Heb. 11:6).

3. *The wall of unyieldingness must be demolished.* Writing to the church at Rome, Paul reminds his readers that he, with them, "received grace . . . for obedience to the faith" (Rom. 1:5). No doubt, he had in mind a moment in his illustrious career when the light of God's revelation broke through to his heart and revealed his own unyieldingness and rebellion against Jesus, whom he had been persecuting. Humbled, in the dust of repentance, he cried, "*Lord*, what do You want me to do?" (Acts 9:6). Later, referring to this heart response, he could testify, "I was not disobedient to the heavenly vision" (Acts 26:19). It is not surprising, therefore, that all through his writings Paul puts great stress on the need for total obedience to the will of God.

God can never fulfill His purpose in our lives while the wall of unyieldingness is still standing.

4. *The wall of unforgiveness must be demolished.* Jesus said: "For if you forgive men their trespasses, your heavenly

Father will also forgive you. But if you do not forgive men their trespasses, neither will your Father forgive your trespasses" (Matt. 6:14–15). I believe that more people are kept out of the full blessing of the gospel of God through unforgiveness than for any other hindrance to salvation. They may be convinced that repentance, faith, and obedience are necessary, but deep down in the heart there is a wall of unforgiveness still standing. A moment's thought on the matter reveals the unreasonableness of this attitude. What right has anyone to expect the forgiveness of God when in that same heart is harbored bitterness, resentment, and unforgivingness against others?

Jesus settled this once and for all when Peter asked: "Lord, how often shall my brother sin against me, and I forgive him? Up to seven times?" Jesus said, "I do not say to you, up to seven times, but up to seventy times seven" (Matt. 18:21–22). Needless to say the Savior's words were intended to convey the thought of unqualified and unconditional forgiveness. At the same time, however, the Master's statement did not (and does not) teach license with God or with man. If we only seek forgiveness in order to sin again, then we show no signs of repentance, or obedience (Rom. 6:1).

It is clear, then, that the walls must be broken down before God can build anew. And interestingly enough, the word for "break down" occurs eight times in the Old Testament, and in each case has reference to the demolition of some wall or hedge. There are, of course, walls of *God's devising* which must be built up around our lives; but here we are talking about the walls of *man's devising* which shut in human sinfulness, and therefore, shut out divine holiness. The Bible insists that without holiness "no one will see the Lord" (Heb. 12:14). Let us see to it, then, that no walls of the old building are left standing. By God's grace let us demolish unbrokenness, unbelief, unyieldingness, and unforgivingness in our lives. Then, and only then, can we face:

The Challenge of God to Establish the New Building

Once again, throughout Holy Scripture, there are many illustrations of the new building which *God* wants to erect in our lives, for we are reminded that "unless the Lord builds the house, they labor in vain who build it" (Ps. 127:1).

Perhaps the most striking passage on the new building that God wants to establish in human experience is found in the Gospel of Luke: "For which of you, intending to build a tower, does not sit down first and count the cost, whether he has enough to finish it—lest, after he has laid the foundation, and is not able to finish, all who see it begin to mock him, saying, 'This man began to build and was not able to finish'" (Luke 14:28–30).

As children, we used to sing:

> We are building day by day,
> At our work and at our play,
> Not with hammer, blow on blow,
> Not with timber sawing so.
> Building a house not made with hands,
> Following Jesus' perfect plans;
> Little builders all are we,
> Building for eternity.
>
> Anonymous

How true it is that we are all building for eternity!

But to stand the test of eternity we need to build aright, and in the verses just quoted, the Lord Jesus teaches us how to build for eternity. First, *the new building must be spiritually conceived.* "Which of you, intending to build a tower, does not sit down first and count the cost, whether he has enough to finish it" (Luke 14:28). Intention presupposes thought, plan, and design. We dare not build for God in a haphazard or fortuitous manner. When Moses was instructed to build the tabernacle, the Lord said unto him, "See that you make all things according to the pattern shown you on the mountain" (Heb. 8:5). The Word of God alone contains the plans of the divine Architect. Unless our conception of what we build finds its authorizations and specifications in the Holy Scriptures, we waste our time on earth and lose our reward in heaven.

Secondly, *the new building must be sacrificially constructed.* "Which of you, intending to build a tower, does not sit down first and count the cost" (Luke 14:28). When the Savior contemplated the cost of building the tower of salvation for men and women, He gave everything—His time, His energy, His body, His life's blood. If you and I are going to build for God, then we shall have to invest everything. It is foolish to begin without counting the cost. The Word of God argues against such a procedure. The work of demolition must be thorough and complete, and the work of building must be just as decisive and disciplined. God wants builders who will labor at any cost.

We must be sure that the *foundation* is right, "for no other foundation can anyone lay than that which is laid, which is Jesus Christ" (1 Cor. 3:11). In terms of personal experience, this means that Christ will be the indwelling controlling presence and power in our lives.

The *materials* must be right. The apostle warns, "Let each one take heed how he builds" (1 Cor. 3:10). If the construction is done in the power of the Holy Spirit, then the materials of gold, silver, and precious stones will be of enduring worth. On the other hand, if the work is being performed in the energy of the flesh, the product of self-effort will be nothing more than wood, hay, and straw (see 1 Cor. 3:12).

Furthermore, the *workmanship* must be right. "Each one's work will become clear; for the Day will declare it, because it will be revealed by fire; and the fire will test each one's work, of what sort it is" (1 Cor. 3:13). It matters not only *what* we build, but *how* we build. The Lord must do it in us and through us, for "unless the Lord builds the house, they labor in vain who build it" (Ps. 127:1).

Thirdly, *the new building must be successfully completed.* "Lest, after he has laid the foundation, and is not able to finish, all who see it begin to mock him, saying, 'This man began to build and was not able to finish'" (Luke 14:29–30). As we ponder these words we are bound to ask ourselves whether they describe the half-built lives and half-finished ministries we see around us today! One of the tragedies within the Christian church is the thousands of so-called believers who represent uncompleted buildings. These people once responded to some special challenge, declaring that they were ready to go anywhere, at any time, at any cost in the service of Jesus Christ, but now they depict the unfulfilled dreams and shattered hopes of "would-be builders." Like Lot's wife, they have refused to go all the way with God, and therefore, have crystallized into monuments of uselessness and shame (Gen. 19:26). Like Ananias and Sapphira, they have held back part of the price and so have been cut off before their life's work was done (Acts 5:1–11). Like Demas, they have loved this present world and so have failed to finish their course (2 Tim. 4:10). If we mean business with God, then we must build by the power of the Spirit to a successful completion. Nothing less than that will merit the Savior's, "Well done, good and faithful servant. . . . Enter into the joy of your lord" (Matt. 25:23).

I have been a pastor; I've also been an evangelist across this country and all over the world. The longer I have lived and the more I have preached, the greater has been my concern for this matter of finishing well. So many people start with a burst of enthusiasm—and that's right and that's healthy. But I often ask the question, "Is that going to be maintained?" It's one thing to start right; it's another to continue in a steadfast fashion, and I say that with deep sincerity. It matters most that we finish right. The apostle Paul could say, "I have fought the good fight, I have finished the race, I have kept the faith"

(2 Tim. 4:7). Only because he could say that, could he add, "There is laid up for me the crown of righteousness, which the Lord, the righteous Judge, will give to me on that Day, and not to me only but also to all who have loved His appearing" (2 Tim. 4:8). You see he wasn't ashamed or afraid to look into the face of his Master and say, "Master, you've chartered my course—I found it; I followed it; I finished it." Did you start well, but lose the goal and the glow? It isn't how you start that matters only, it isn't only how you continue, but how you finish. You are called to endure, and to endure until the end. Are you prepared to look into your Savior's face this very moment and say, "Lord Jesus, keep me faithful until the very end." How true, then, are the words that there is "a time to break down, and a time to build up" (Eccl. 3:3). If the demolishing has been done, and done well, then you are ready to build. Or, more accurately, God is building in you and through you by the power of the Holy Spirit. Yes, there is a challenge—the challenge of God to demolish the old building and establish the new building. Are you and I prepared to break down walls of pride, unbelief, disobedience, and unforgivingness in order that in us may be born a faith which counts upon God to build "a house not made with hands, eternal in the heavens" (2 Cor. 5:1)? If the answer is yes, then let us enlist in God's program and make sure that day by day we count upon Him to build brick upon brick with such precision, such conviction that when the storm comes we will find ourselves unshaken. Remember the words of the Lord Jesus, "A wise man . . . built his house on the rock" (Matt. 7:24).

Think on These Things (Phil. 4:8)

As I watched a bulldozer clear the ground for our "Vision 2000" ministry center here in Memphis, Tennessee, I cringed with pain and sadness as I saw big and beautiful trees go down one after another. Several months later, however, it was another story! A magnificent building emerged on that same piece of land. There was a "time to break down," and in due time, "there was a time to build up." True brokenness and repentance always cause heart-pain and contrition, but on that foundation God builds His "kingdom which cannot be shaken" (Heb. 12:28).

A Time to Weep
And a Time to Laugh

*A*nyone who loves great hymns will know of the compositions of Anne Steele. As a child, she had an accident that made her an invalid for life. In her late teens, when she seemed to have partially conquered her physical problems, she was introduced to Mr. Ellscourt, and they soon fell in love. Her cup of joy overflowed when he asked her to be his wife. But on the wedding day, as she eagerly awaited his arrival, a messenger came with the tragic news that he had drowned. Stunned with grief, she retired to her room to weep and seek comfort from God's Word. Recovering her strength, she wrote a hymn that has brought healing to many a wounded spirit:

Father, whate'er of earthly bliss
Thy sovereign will denies,
Accepted at Thy throne of grace
Let this petition rise:
Give me a calm and thankful heart,
From every murmur free,
The blessings of Thy grace impart,
And let me live to Thee.

Miss Steele wrote the lyrics for 144 other sacred songs, even though she spent the last nine years of her life as a shut-in (Bosch 1976). To study her life is to know what it is to reflect and radiate the Spirit of the indwelling Christ, for it is clear that Jesus had this capacity to weep and to laugh. We read that there were times when He "rejoiced in the Spirit" (Luke 10:21). People saw the merry twinkle in His eyes and heard the laughter in His voice. Then at other times He was truly the "Man of sorrows and acquainted with grief" (Is. 53:3). As we shall see presently, He wept at the graveside of a dear friend; He wept as He surveyed a shepherdless multitude; He wept over a city that had lost its soul. So there is a time to weep, just as there is a time to laugh. Reverently, we need to examine these God-given capacities.

The Capacity for Tearfulness

There is a popular notion that tears are associated *only* with having a fallen nature and living a life of sin, but the teaching of Scripture does not bear this out. Our Lord and Savior was neither fallen in His nature or sinful in His living, yet He wept. In His humanity, God had given Him a capacity for tearfulness, and so in this sense there is a place for holy tears. And, of course, the converse is just as true. Because of our sin, fallen man can shed and must shed tears of remorse, of bitterness, and even of hardened rebellion. Hell is described as a place of "weeping and gnashing of teeth" (Matt. 8:12).

In our consideration of this capacity for tearfulness, however, we are restricting ourselves to the two positive aspects
of weeping. First of all, there is the shedding of *natural tears*.
Because we are human, there are times in life when we can do
nothing other than shed tears. For example, there is the sorrow of parting, such as Timothy felt when Paul was arrested
and taken away from him. Writing later to his son in the faith,
Paul could say, "[I] greatly [desire] to see you, being mindful
of your tears, that I may be filled with joy" (2 Tim. 1:4). We
recall how the Ephesian elders wept as they bade the apostle
farewell for the last time (Acts 20:37). There is also the sorrow of bereavement, as when Jesus cried at the graveside of
Lazarus (John 11:35). Then, of course, there is the sorrow of
our mortality, when we sense the frailty of our bodies and
groan and long to be delivered (Rom. 8:22; 2 Cor. 5:2). This
sense of our creatureliness finds expression in many forms
throughout the pilgrimage of life. It was this kind of experience that made the Psalmist pray, "Put my tears into Your
bottle" (Ps. 56:8). As a minister, I have shed natural tears
many times because of the suffering and bereavement of my
people. Not to be able to weep on occasions like this is to be
insensitive, abnormal, and lacking in the God-given capacity
for tearfulness.

But with natural tears, there are also the *spiritual tears*. In
an article entitled "When Should a Christian Weep?" John
R. W. Stott (1969, 107–108) reminds us that there are some
salutary things that need special attention in this superficial
age in which we live. He says: "Evangelism has been debased
into the simple invitation to 'come to Jesus and be happy.' The
signature tune of the Christian Church has been 'I am *Happy*.'
Christians are to appear hearty, ebullient and boisterous." He
continues: "In a Christian magazine I receive, every Christian's picture (and there are many) shows him with a grin from
ear to ear. Some Christians," he maintains, "would defend this
attitude by quoting such [a] Scripture as 'Rejoice in the Lord

always.'" But this is not "the true biblical image of the Christian." Our pattern is Jesus "who went about saying, 'Be of cheer . . . Go in peace,' yet was called 'the Man of sorrows.' The apostle Paul expressed the same paradox [when he declared], 'as sorrowful, yet always rejoicing.'"

Spiritual tears are *tears of contrition*. We all know the story of the woman who stood behind Jesus weeping, and then began to wash His feet with her tears (Luke 7:38). Those were tears of repentance for her sin and gratitude for her forgiveness. Would to God we saw more "holy water" of this kind in our gospel meetings!

I once remember hearing Duncan Campbell say that he doubted the reality of any man's conversion who had not wept over his sins.

David Brainerd, that most saintly missionary to the Indians at the beginning of the eighteenth century, could write in his diary for Oct 18, 1740:

> In my morning devotions my soul was exceedingly melted, and I bitterly mourned over my great sinfulness and vileness. I never before had felt so pungent and deep a sense of the odious nature of sin, as this time. My soul was then unusually carried forth in love to God, and had a lively sense of God's love to me. (Stott 1969, 108)

God give us more men and tears like this!

Spiritual tears are *tears of compassion*. It is recorded that when the Lord Jesus "saw the multitudes, He was moved with compassion for them, because they were weary and scattered, like sheep having no shepherd" (Matt. 9:36). The sight of scattered sheep without a shepherd wrung His heart and He could not withhold His tears. In like manner, He wept over a city, crying: "O Jerusalem, Jerusalem, the one who kills the prophets and stones those who are sent to her! How often I wanted to gather your children together, as a hen gathers her chicks under her wings, but you were not willing! See! Your house is left to you desolate" (Matt. 23:37–38). The apostle Paul possessed this capacity for tearfulness. He could write: "I tell the truth in Christ, I am not lying, my conscience also bearing me witness in the Holy Spirit, that I have great sorrow and continual grief in my heart. For I could wish that I myself were accursed from Christ for my brethren, my countrymen according to the flesh" (Rom. 9:1–3). The burden of his unsaved Hebrew friends weighed so heavily upon him that day and night he shed prayerful tears for them.

Bishop J. C. Ryle once said of George Whitefield that the people "could not hate the man who wept so much over their souls." Andrew Bonar wrote in his diary on his 49th birthday: "Felt in the evening most bitter grief over the apathy of the district. They are perishing, they are perishing, and yet they will not consider. I lay awake thinking over and crying to the Lord in broken groans." We are told that that great theologian and preacher, Dr. R. W. Dale of Birmingham, was at first critical of D. L. Moody's preaching until he went to hear him. Thereafter, he had the most profound respect for the evangelist because he said Moody "could never speak of a lost soul without tears in his eyes" (Stott 1969, 109).

Spiritual tears are *tears of concern*. Compassion and concern must not be confused. Without doubt there is no true compassion without concern, but concern may not evoke compassion. On the contrary, concern may lead to holy jealousy, righteous indignation, and social action. The Psalmist could admit, "Rivers of water run down from my eyes, because men do not keep Your law" (Psalm 119:136). And it was this kind of concern that led Paul to say to the Philippians that there were many whom he could only mention with tears because they were "the enemies of the cross of Christ" (Phil. 3:18).

Alas, we have become so immune to the challenge of social evils, that we can read headlines, listen to news reports, and watch gruesome pictures on the television screen without

batting an eyelid. I don't believe God will ever hear our prayers
for the troubles of the world until we know how to weep. Indeed, I don't believe God will ever intervene on behalf of our
own country until the social evils that besmirch our land drive
the church to her knees and to tears.

So there is a time to weep, and God has given all normal
people capacity for tearfulness.

But to balance this truth we must consider also:

The Capacity for Cheerfulness

In the article by John Stott already referred to, he quotes Dr.
W. E. Sangster's story of a very highbrow organist who
pleaded with the drummer in the Salvation Army band not to
hit the drum so hard. The beaming bandsman replied, "Lor'
bless you, sir, since I've been converted I'm so happy I could
bust the bloomin' drum."

There is a time to laugh, and there are two aspects of such
laughter. There is *the natural cheerfulness*. Someone has pointed
out that it takes a good laugh to exercise the entire complement of muscles that surround the face and throat of a normal
person. Dr. G. Campbell Morgan (1934, 51) says, "The power
to laugh, to cease work, and frolic in forgetfulness of all the
conflict, to make merry, is a divine bestowment upon man."
Natural cheerfulness is usually associated with *the happy Spirit*.
The Scripture says, "A merry heart does good, like medicine"
(Prov. 17:22), and again, "A merry heart makes a cheerful
countenance, . . . he who is of a merry heart has a continual
feast" (Prov. 15:13, 15). Nothing is more scintillating and up-
lifting than to be around a person possessed of a happy disposition.

Then, so often, natural cheerfulness comes from the *humorous story*. Thank God for those whose wit and mental abil-
ity have a humorous turn. All of us enjoy listening to a good
storyteller who can draw forth laughter with good taste and
timing. So there is natural cheerfulness.

But even more important, there is *the spiritual cheerfulness*. The gospel is the glad "tidings of great joy" (Luke 2:10), and in God's presence there is "fullness of joy" (Ps. 16:11). Indeed, Jesus wanted His disciples to be full of joy (John 15:11; 16:24; 17:13), and we are reminded by the apostle Paul that "the fruit of the Spirit is . . . joy" (Gal. 5:22). But we must be sure what we mean by such joy.

The Bible teaches that true joy is the expression of a deep spiritual experience with God. There is *the joy of Christian forgiveness*. "Therefore, having been justified by faith, we have peace with God through our Lord Jesus Christ, through whom also we have access by faith into this grace in which we stand, and rejoice in hope of the glory of God" (Rom. 5:1–2). David could express the same sentiment when he exclaimed, "Blessed [happy] is he whose transgression is forgiven, whose sin is covered" (Ps. 32:1). No one can know real joy without the forgiveness of sin. True, there is a happiness that is artificial and synthetic, but cheerfulness is the refracted light of the inward lamp of joy.

The story is told of a famous comedian who came to see a psychiatrist. He was suffering from deep depression and heaviness of spirit. He confessed that there was no joy in his life and that life was a hollow thing. Without knowing the significance of what he was saying, the psychiatrist suggested that among other things he should go to a certain theater and listen to the starring comedian. After a deathly pause, the man looked up into the face of the psychiatrist and said, "I am that comedian!"

Do you and I know the joy and blessedness of sins forgiven? We will never be able to laugh as God intended until we know that the blood of Christ has covered the guilt of sin and that the grip of sin has been conquered by the power of Christ.

There is also *the joy of Christian fellowship*. In the greatest chapter on fellowship in the Bible, John the apostle says,

"Truly our fellowship is with the Father and with His Son Jesus Christ. And these things we write to you that your joy may be full" (1 John 1:3–4). Outside of the forgiveness of sin there is no joy quite like the joy of Christian fellowship. Listen to Christians as they gather at a time of conference, or around a meal table, or at a cozy fireside! The laughter you hear at such times is both holy and healthy. There is nothing phony about it; it is the true expression of Christian cheerfulness. Whatever the world may say about the failures and foibles of the church of Jesus Christ, it is still the greatest and most joyous fellowship on earth!

Most importantly, there is *the joy of Christian fulfillment.* It is said that the Lord Jesus "for the joy that was set before Him endured the cross, despising the shame, and has sat down at the right hand of the throne of God" (Heb. 12:2). To Him, there was no greater joy than that of fulfilling the will of God. Throughout His life He was forever saying, "My food is to do the will of Him who sent Me, and to finish His work" (John 4:34). And this was because His joy, or delight, was ever to do the will of God.

Show me a person who is in the center of God's will and fulfilling the Lord's commission, and I will introduce you to someone who has a capacity for cheerfulness. There is something exhilarating and exciting about working for Jesus. There is a fulfillment in Christian service that cannot be found anywhere else in the world. And when I talk about Christian service I do not necessarily refer to what is commonly known as "full-time Christian service." Wonderful as it is to be set apart for a specific God-given task, we must not overlook the fact that the housewife, the banker, the college professor, or the factory worker can serve Jesus Christ just as devotedly and hilariously as the missionary on the foreign field.

So we have seen that there is "a time to weep," (Eccl. 3:4) and God sees our tears and shares our tears. Do you share the tears of a broken world? How many members of your family are hurting, and you don't know anything about it? It may be even closer than that—your husband, wife, children, or parents may have a deep grief in their heart because of something that has happened to them. You may be going in and out of the house and be as cold, calculated, and clinical as the "professional" man. Do you suffer with your family? What about your church? Do you know that in every church there are broken hearts? I have been a pastor long enough to know that I never stand in the pulpit without knowing that I look into the faces of people who are crying inside. That is why in my pastoral prayers, and I trust in my preaching and in counseling, I always seek to identify with suffering hearts? What about people in your church who are really hurting? Do you identify with them? Do you seek them out? Do you know that the Bible says, "if one member suffers, all the members suffer" (1 Cor. 12:26). That is to say that nobody can be suffering in any given church without others feeling it, unless their sensitivities have been dulled. If we are answering to the Headship of Christ as our Lord, and the Holy Spirit is truly witnessing in our hearts to all that is going on in a local church, then we won't rest until we seek out those who need tenderness, consideration, and love.

But there is also "a time to laugh," (Eccl. 3:4) and God is just as much in our cheers as He is in our tears. Do you enjoy fun with others? Do you enjoy fellowship in the home and the church? There is no better representative of Christianity than a happy Christian. Joy is the flag that flutters at the mast of the castle when King Jesus is in residence. Unfortunately, most people see our flag flying at half-mast! Do you know what it is to rejoice in the little things? Geoffrey King recalls the story of a newly converted boy in a missionary school in India. The little lad was an excellent soccer player, and a day or two after his encounter with the Lord, he was on the field playing hard at the game. Presently he received a pass, and dribbling the ball through the defense, he delivered a glorious shot. Just as the ball was passing through the goalposts he was heard by one of the staff to say, "Look, Jesus, it's a goal! It's a goal!" So real was the relationship of this boy to his Savior that he was determined to share the joy of that moment. I can't help feeling that there was laughter in heaven, even as there was delight in the heart of that lad.

Think on These Things (Phil. 4:8)

There is "a time to weep" and there is "a time to laugh" (Eccl. 3:4). Do we have this God-given capacity for tearfulness and cheerfulness? To have it is to know the spirit of Jesus who said, "Blessed are those who mourn, for they shall be comforted" (Matt. 5:4). Someone has said that "tears are the lenses through which our dim eyes see more deeply into heaven and look more fully upon [the face of God]" (Miller 1912, April 17). And the wonderful thing about it is that as we see this vision of the face of God our hearts are filled with "joy inexpressible and full of glory" (1 Pet. 1:8). Let us live with "a tear in one eye and a twinkle in the other."

7

A Time to Mourn
And a Time to Dance

Some of the greatest lessons I have ever learned have been learned at funerals and weddings. It is quite amazing how human characteristics surface on occasions like this. Was the Preacher thinking of these two experiences of life when he wrote, "There is . . . a time to mourn, and a time to dance"? (Eccl. 3:1, 4). Who has not found time to weep and mourn? The Bible says, "Man is born to trouble, as the sparks fly upward" (Job 5:7; see also 14:1). And yet so often lesson after lesson is needed to make us realize that this world is a vale of tears. We look everywhere to avoid this or that trouble, but without success. Even for the Christian, sorrow and suffering are inescapable. Jesus said, "In the world you will have tribulation" (John 16:33). But the darkest side of the Canaan road is brighter than the light of a thousand worlds, for God has promised to turn our "mourning into dancing" (Ps. 30:11) and to fill our mouths "with laughter, and our tongue with singing" (Ps. 126:2). So Solomon was right when he wrote, "There is . . . a time to mourn, and a time to dance" (Eccl. 3:1, 4).

Even at first glance it is obvious that this couplet is closely related to the one we considered in our last study. "A time to weep, and a time to laugh" intimates the spontaneous manifestation of the feelings of the heart; "a time to mourn, and a time to dance" is the more formal expression of these same feelings, as performed at funerals, weddings, and similar occasions. The contrast between mourning and dancing is found in our Lord's allusion to the sulky children in the marketplace who would not join their companions in play. Addressing His listeners, the Lord Jesus said: "To what shall I liken this generation? It is like children sitting in the marketplaces and calling to their companions, and saying: 'We played the flute for you, and you did not dance; we mourned to you, and you did not lament'" (Matt. 11:16–17). The Master's intention, as the context shows, was to strike at the lack of repentance on the part of the people, and therefore, the absence of the true joy which comes through the forgiveness of sin and the favor of God.

To understand the deeper implications of mourning and dancing we must start with:

The Spirit of Brokenness

One of the greatest needs of our day is for old-time conviction of sin; and one of the purposes for which the Holy Spirit was sent down from heaven on the day of Pentecost was to engender this conviction in the hearts of men and women. The Lord Jesus predicted this when He announced: "He will convict the world of sin, and of righteousness, and of judgment: of sin, because they do not believe in Me; of righteousness, because I go to My Father and you see Me no more; of judgment, because the ruler of this world is judged" (John 16:8–11). Until men and women know the meaning of mourning they will never know the meaning of dancing, and such mourning comes about when the Holy Spirit convicts men and women of *the consciousness of sin*. "For all have sinned and fall short of the glory of God" (Rom. 3:23). Literally this means that all have *consciously* sinned. Job was conscious of his sin when he cried, "Behold, I am vile" (Job 40:4). Isaiah was conscious of his sin when he said, "Woe is me, for I am undone!" (Is. 6:5). Peter was conscious of his sin when he exclaimed, "Depart from me, for I am a sinful man, O Lord!" (Luke 5:8). Paul was conscious of his sin when he wrote, "O wretched man that I am! Who will deliver me?" (Rom. 7:24).

Some time ago an assassination attempt was made on the life of Gerald Ford, then President of the United States of America. In reporting this event, an Associated Press release stated: "A psychiatric examination has been ordered for the woman who says she 'willfully and knowingly' attempted to kill President Ford. She said she was ready to answer for her act." The article went on to say that a U.S. District Judge had told her, "If you enter this plea of guilty, there is a possibility you can be sent to jail for life." Her reply was that she could see no "reasonable [and] honorable" way of avoiding it. "There comes a point," she declared, "when we each have to answer to ourselves, and it is with our own conscience that we must make peace."

"The woman's sanity was questioned because she admitted her guilt. Granted, a number of factors in her past behavior may have prompted the reaction to her confession. But the general implication was that her open acknowledgment of wrongdoing, rather than the customary denial, was what called for the mental tests" (De Haan 1976). Isn't it amazing how modern man with all his sophistication, dodges the issue of true conviction of sin. Just because this woman realized her sin and wished to confess it, she was told she needed a mental test!

Sigmund Freud, the Austrian scientist and psychologist, despite his anti-religious prejudices, once said, "Original sin is a fact, since psychoanalysis has revealed a whole world of rottenness and villainy which had not been hitherto suspected by psychologists, even though its presence was clearly enough attested by the New Testament."

But the Holy Spirit not only convicts of the consciousness of sin, but also of the *culpability of sin*. "For all have sinned and fall short of the glory of God" (Rom. 3:23). This means that the Spirit of God reveals to us the fact that we have failed to meet God's holy standards. Such a falling short of the mark brings us to a sense of guilt and culpability. Emil Brunner says, "The Christian conception of radical evil is this: it is radical sin. As a sinner, man is not confronted with an impersonal law of good, but with the will of the Creator" (1942, 142). In the ultimate sense, therefore, however much we may affect others in the process, we actually sin against God. David knew this when he confessed, "Against You, You only, have I sinned, and done this evil in Your sight" (James 1:15).

But even more than this, the Holy Spirit convicts of *the consequences of sin*. "Some men's sins are clearly evident, preceding them to judgment, but those of some men follow later" (1 Tim. 5:24). Oh, the effects of our sins! Think of the spoiled characters, the seared consciences, and the social conflicts that follow upon a life of sinfulness. The Bible tells us that "the wages of sin is death" (Rom. 6:23), and again, "When desire has conceived, it gives birth to sin; and sin, when it is full-grown, brings forth death" (Rom. 6:23).

Have we ever considered the *death* wounds that we can inflict upon the lives of men and women, not to mention our own? Think of those searching words of James, the brother of our Lord. "Where do wars and fights come from among you? Do they not come from your desires for pleasure that war in your members? You lust and do not have. You murder and covet and cannot obtain. You fight and war. Yet you do not have because you do not ask" (James 4:1–2). He is saying that the consequences of lust and sin are nothing less than war and death. Let us remember that there is more than one way of killing a person. There is, of course, physical death; but what shall we say of the death of honor, the death of reputation, the death of purity, the death of spiritual values?

It is because of these consequences of sin that James proceeds to call his readers to repentance and mourning. He writes: "Draw near to God and He will draw near to you. Cleanse your hands, you sinners; and purify your hearts, you double-minded. Lament and mourn and weep! Let your laughter be turned to mourning and your joy to gloom. Humble yourselves in the sight of the Lord, and He will lift you up" (James 4:8–10). Until we know how to mourn over the consciousness, culpability, and consequences of our sin we shall never know how to dance. Until we know how to humble ourselves under the mighty hand of God we shall never know what it is to be exalted in due season (1 Peter 5:6). There must be brokenness before there can be blessedness. The Psalmist reminds us, "The sacrifices of God are a broken spirit, a broken and a contrite heart—these, O God, You will not despise" (Ps. 51:17).

Such brokenness leads to:

The Spirit of Blessedness

The term "dancing" has no reference whatsoever to worldly amusements. The Scriptures restrict the concept of dancing to the exercise of religious worship (Ex. 15:20; 2 Sam. 6:14–16; Ps. 30:11–12). The word signifies "to leap for great joy," and indicates praise to God, accompanied by singing or music. In the Old Testament, dancing was associated with the crossing of the Red Sea, military victories, and religious festivals (Ex. 15:20; 1 Sam. 18:6; Judg. 21:19–21). In the New Testament, when the apostle Paul had to rebuke the Corinthian church for not defending his divine authority (2 Cor. 7:8–13), under attack by "an evil intruder," the leadership responded with "godly sorrow [that produced] repentance leading to salvation, not to be regretted" (2 Cor. 7:10). This made Paul happy. He writes: "Now I rejoice [dance in my heart!] . . . that your sorrow [has] led to repentance" (2 Cor. 7:9).

Again and again we read of God giving repentance to those who turn from their wicked ways and trust in the Lord Jesus Christ. Peter could say after the day of Pentecost, "The God of our fathers raised up Jesus. . . . [and] has exalted [Him] to His right hand to be Prince and Savior, to give repentance to Israel and forgiveness of sins" (Acts 5:30–31). He could also report how God had *granted* to the Gentiles "repentance to life" (Acts 11:18).

If we want to know the spirit of blessedness, we must ask God for true repentance. Only then will our mourning be turned into dancing. The reason why we don't know the joy of the Lord in our lives is that we are unwilling to pay the price of repentance. So often we relegate that term repentance to the unconverted. It's the world who needs to repent, we say. But repentance is a word that is also used for Christians. Read the messages of the risen Lord to the seven churches. To five out of the seven He employs the word "repent" or "repentance." "Judgment [must] begin at the house of God" (1 Pet. 4:17). Before there can be blessedness, there must be brokenness.

With the blessedness of divine repentance, there is also *the blessedness of divine acceptance.* In the 30th Psalm, David describes a mighty experience of deliverance from sin when he senses the favor of divine acceptance and concludes by saying, "You have turned for me my mourning into dancing; You have put off my sackcloth and clothed me with gladness, to the end that my glory may sing praise to You and not be silent. O Lord my God, I will give thanks to You forever" (Ps. 30:11–12).

The New Testament version of this is found in that immortal story of the restored prodigal son. Never did a young man mourn for his sins like that lad sitting in the pigsty of a far country! But having truly repented, he returned to his father and "when he was still a great way off, his father saw him and had compassion, and ran and fell on his neck and kissed him" (Luke 15:20). Was language ever more descriptive of divine acceptance? That boy received the kiss of forgiveness, the robe of respectability, the ring of affection, and the shoes of reinstatement. But that was not all. A feast was spread for the converted boy, and friends and neighbors were invited to eat and be merry. And we read that there was "music and dancing"! (Luke 15:25). When the father was asked by the elder brother to explain the reason for the music and dancing, he replied, "It was right that we should make merry and be glad, for your brother was dead and is alive again, and was lost and is found" (Luke 15:32).

Has dancing started in our hearts? If not, it is because we have never known the experience of mourning for our sins. But when there is true Holy Spirit-brokenness, there will always be true Holy Spirit-blessedness.

How true, then, are the words, "There is . . . a time to mourn, and a time to dance" (Eccl. 3:1, 4). There is a time for funerals and there is a time for weddings. The greatest funeral any one of us can attend is the funeral of death to self and sin in order that we might live unto God. This is a costly business, and it involves genuine mourning; but when the funeral is over, a wedding immediately follows! We are "married to another" (Rom. 7:4), to Jesus Christ our Lord, and then the dancing begins and never ends.

So we close as we started: "There is . . . a time to mourn, and a time to dance" (Eccl. 3:1, 4). Jesus said, "Blessed are those who mourn, for they shall be comforted" (Matt. 5:4). This comfort is the blessedness of *the Father's pardon*. Paul speaks of "the Father of mercies and God of all comfort" (2 Cor. 1:3). The Father's comfort is based upon His pardoning mercies. Mercy is divine love in action, extended to the undeserving. Oh, the comfort, of knowing that God, in mercy, has extended His pardon to such miserable sinners as you and me! God always takes cognizance of those who mourn and weep on account of their sins and has promised the comfort of His mercy and forgiveness.

This comfort is the blessedness *of the Savior's peace*. Right through the Messianic prophecies Jesus is spoken of as the comfort of His people: "'Comfort, yes, comfort My people!' says your God" (Is. 40:1). In Luke 2:25 we are told that the just and devout Simeon waited for "the Consolation Israel." Nor was he disappointed, for the day came when it was revealed to him by the Holy Spirit that he should not see death until he had seen the Lord's Christ. "So he came by the Spirit into the temple. And when the parents brought in the Child Jesus, . . . he took Him up in his arms and blessed God and said: 'Lord, now You are letting Your servant depart in peace, according to Your word; for my eyes have seen Your salvation'" (Luke 2:27–30). Ever since then, men, women, boys and girls, all over the world have embraced the same Jesus and found the comfort of His peace, "which surpasses all understanding" (Phil. 4:7). Do you know anything of that comfort in your life? It comes only to those who mourn. This comfort is the blessedness of *the Spirit's power*. Before the Lord Jesus left for heaven, He gathered His disciples around Him and said, "I will pray the Father, and He will give you another Helper [Comforter], that He may abide with you forever" (John 14:16). What could have been more empowering to the disciples than these words? Later, speaking of the same Spirit, the Master declared, "You shall receive power when the Holy Spirit has come upon you" (Acts 1:8). This comforting power was the secret of their courage in times of opposition, and confidence in times of tribulation. The same Comforter is with us today, but His power to fill, strengthen, and empower God's people is dependent upon the spirit of brokenness and yieldedness in our lives. Indeed, the blessedness of the comfort of pardon, peace, and power from God the Father, God the Son, and God the Spirit is only for those who mourn.

Have you paid the price of true repentance in your life? Have you ever knelt and said, "Lord Jesus, I want you to break this stubborn will of mine. I want to bring my entire life under submission to your Lordship, so that the Holy Spirit may fill me with the Father's pardon, the Savior's peace, and the Spirit's power"? Only when this happens will we "dance" in our hearts. Only the Holy Spirit can give us a light in our eyes, a lilt in our voice, and a spring in our step. People will see us walking across the stage of life as those who are "dancing" in the most sanctified sense of that term, alive to God and aware of the world in which we have to live and serve.

So we have seen that the spirit of brokenness is the pathway to spiritual blessedness. Only as we mourn will we dance. Daniel Iverson (1963) knew this principle when he wrote:

> Spirit of the living God, fall fresh on me.
> Spirit of the living God, fall fresh on me.
> Melt me, mold me, fill me, use me.
> Spirit of the living God, fall fresh on me.

Think on These Things (Phil. 4:8)

The East African revival is generally acknowledged as one of the longest and most remarkable of any spiritual awakening on that continent, or anywhere else in the world. One of the best-known leaders in that spiritual movement was Bishop Festo Kivengere. I once asked him to give me the secret of the longevity and vitality of the revival. His reply was simple, yet powerful. He said, "Two characteristics of the revival were brokenness and walking in the light." Brokenness is willingness to mourn over our sins and seek cleansing and restoration. Walking in the light is restored fellowship with God and fellow believers—issuing in joy and dancing! Daily obedience to these two Biblical principles determines personal revival and pervasive revival.

8

A Time to Cast Away Stones and a Time to Gather Stones

I enjoy gardens! When I had a pastorate in London, England, I never tired of walking through the botanical gardens at Kew in Surrey. This was only a few minutes walk from our home. The variety of trees and plants, the gorgeous display of flowers, and the peacefulness of the surroundings were a benediction to my soul. Time and time again I was "lost in wonder, love, and praise."

I can understand why the healthy Christian life is likened to a garden. Isaiah the prophet speaks of the child of God as "a watered garden, . . . a spring of water, whose waters do not fail" (Is. 58:11). Do you identify with those words, or is your life cluttered up with stones and rubbish?

A careful study of our text in the light of related passages makes evident that the writer has in mind the operation of clearing a vineyard of stones and of collecting materials for making fences, winepresses, and towers. Isaiah has the same idea when, in the parable of Jehovah's vineyard, he writes: "My Well-beloved has a vineyard on a very fruitful hill. He dug it up and cleared out its stones, and planted it with the choicest vine. He built a tower in its midst, and also made a winepress in it; so He expected it to bring forth good grapes, but it brought forth wild grapes" (Is. 5:1–2).

Three times in the history of the world God has made a vineyard for Himself, with the expectation of receiving fruit for His glory. The first was the vineyard of a human paradise. Man was put in the Garden of Eden with the mandate to "tend and keep it" (Gen. 2:15). But we all know the story of his failure to produce the fruit that God expected. Through disobedience, sin not only affected every area of his own life, but also cursed the whole human race. The second was the vineyard of the Hebrew people. Isaiah tells us about this in the passage that we have already quoted. God did everything to ensure that this vineyard would produce the best of fruit for His honor—but, instead, "it brought forth wild grapes" (Is. 5:2). The third is the vineyard of the Christian church. Jesus Himself came to plant this garden and declared: "I am the true vine, and My Father is the vinedresser. Every branch in Me that does not bear fruit He takes away; and every branch that bears fruit He prunes, that it may bear more fruit" (John 15:1–2). Once again, the church has, in generation after generation, failed to fulfill the ultimate purpose of God. But such is the sovereignty and persistence of our loving God that He will not let us go. And so he continues to speak to us, and strive with us, until the day when the church will be presented "before the presence of His glory with exceeding joy" (Jude 24).

This, then, is the message of our text. It is the picture of a neglected and fruitless vineyard. In such a situation two major operations are called for, the first of which is:

The Cultivation of the Vineyard of Our Lives

In olden times it was not an uncommon thing to find a vineyard that had suffered through enemy attack or through willful neglect. And without doubt, Solomon had this in mind as he surveys a promising piece of land, strewn with stones and debris. In circumstances like this, there comes "a time to cast away stones" (Eccl. 3:5).

What is true in this physical sense is even more relevant when we think of the vineyard of our lives. *We must admit the presence of stones in our lives.* In this connection, there is a revealing passage in Proverbs 24:30–34, which reads:

> I went by the field of the lazy man, and by the vineyard of the man devoid of understanding; and there it was, all overgrown with thorns; its surface was covered with nettles; its stone wall was broken down. When I saw it, I considered it well; I looked on it and received instruction: a little sleep, a little slumber, a little folding of the hands to rest; so shall your poverty come like a prowler, and your need like an armed man.

Stones, in and of themselves, constitute valuable material, as we shall see later. But stones scattered in this fashion represent thoughtlessness, carelessness, and laziness.

There is first of all *thoughtlessness.* Solomon tells us that a yard in this state belongs, of necessity, to "the man devoid of understanding" (Prov. 24:30). A life that is not fulfilling the purpose of God is the life of a person who has ceased to use his intelligence. There is nothing clever or commendable about young people, or older ones, who through recklessness and rash decisions have allowed their lives to go to pieces. God gave us minds to think His thoughts after Him, and everything He has designed for us is summed up in the Supreme Thought, even Jesus Christ our Lord. This is why the Lord Jesus was forever inviting people to come to Him, learn of Him, and follow Him.

Also, there is *carelessness*—"And there it was, all overgrown with thorns; its surface was covered with nettles; its stone wall was broken down" (Prov. 24:31). What a graphic picture this is of willful neglect. Think of the thorns, the nettles, and the stone wall broken down. Does this represent our hearts, our lives, our vineyards? Thorns and nettles are symbols of the curse, while the broken wall is the evidence of capitulation to enemy attack. "He who digs a pit will fall into it, and whoever breaks through a wall will be bitten by a serpent" (Eccl. 10:8). When we allow the wall of our lives to be penetrated by the "subtle serpent," the inevitable results follow: thorns, nettles, and scattered stones.

Then, there is *laziness*—"When I saw it, I considered it well; I looked on it and received instruction: a little sleep, a little slumber, a little folding of the hands to rest; so shall your poverty come like a prowler, and your need like an armed man" (Prov. 24:32–34). It was D. L. Moody who used to say that no regenerate man should have a drop of lazy blood in his veins. Laziness is the result of the curse, and there is plenty of evidence of that curse in our modern life! This is why homes are divided, businesses are corrupted, and the world is in such a mess. People want their own easy way of self-seeking and sinfulness, and so the vineyard of the Lord is reduced to thorns, nettles, and rubble. The only way to reverse the situation is to admit the presence of these stones in our lives. Are we guilty of thoughtlessness, carelessness, and laziness? We must remember that this is nothing less than sin, and sin must be dealt with at the cross of Calvary. Is that garden life of yours a mess? Is it full of rubble and debris? Is it less than what God intended? Thank God, the stones can be cleared away—"If we confess our sins, He is faithful and just to forgive us our sins and to cleanse us from all unrighteousness" (1 John 1:9).

But it is not sufficient to admit the presence of stones in our lives; *we must permit the clearance of stones in our lives*. When the condition of our lives is revealed to us through the preaching of the Word of God and the searching of the Spirit of God, we must be willing for these stones to be removed. This will call for humbleness, prayerfulness, and steadfastness. No one can pick up stones without bending down, and this is the only place where God meets us: at the cross of His blessed Son. This is *humbleness.* Then it is evident that no one can pick up stones without securely holding them in their hands, and the very action of lifting these stones is the posture of *prayerfulness.* We must ask God to deal with our sins, to cleanse our lives, and to renew our spirits. And then it goes without saying that picking up stones is an arduous task; it is heavy work. It calls for *steadfastness.* You have to be willing to drop on your knees, pick up those stones, present them, and say, "Here they are Lord. These are the sins that are spoiling my garden life." Then as you hold them before Him, confess those sins. As we have already remarked, "He is faithful and just to forgive us our sins and to cleanse us from all unrighteousness" (1 John 1:9). Then follows steadfastness, for it is hard work. In presenting the gospel, our Lord Jesus and His apostles always insisted on this characteristic of obedience and steadfast continuance. Jesus said, "If anyone desires to come after Me, let him deny himself, and *take up his cross daily, and follow Me*" (Luke 9:23). The apostles exhorted their converts "that with purpose of heart they should continue with the Lord" (Acts 11:23). And it is recorded that the early disciples "continued steadfastly in the apostles' doctrine and fellowship, in the breaking of bread, and in prayers" (Acts 2:42). God will never take us seriously until we take Him seriously.

This, then, constitutes the cultivation of the vineyard of our lives. We must admit the presence of the stones, and then permit the clearance of those stones. Only thus will our lives become the fruitful land for God to work, by the power of His Spirit. What He is looking for in our lives is *fruitfulness.* Over fifty times in the New Testament the subject of fruitfulness is mentioned. And the Lord Jesus reminded His disciples before He went to heaven that "by this My Father is glorified, that you bear much fruit" (John 15:8). Not just fruit, but "much fruit." It is the "much fruit" that glorifies our Father which is in heaven. Remember that "man's chief end is to glorify God and to enjoy Him forever" (Westminster Shorter Catechism). There is no other purpose for your creation, preservation, and redemption than that you should glorify the Father.

A missionary was visited by a Korean convert who had walked 100 miles to learn more about Jesus. After giving his testimony, the young man recited the entire Sermon on the Mount without making a mistake. The missionary was delighted, but felt he ought to warn him that memorizing the Bible is not enough. Its precepts must be put into practice. When he made this suggestion, the Korean's face lit up with a happy smile. "That's the way I learned it," he said. "When I first tried to master that long passage, it just wouldn't stick in my mind. So I decided to grasp just one verse at a time and then follow its instructions as I lived among my friends and neighbors. When I saw how well it worked, I had no difficulty remembering it, and I could go on to the next beatitude." The young believer had discovered a significant principle: the admonitions of God's Word become firmly embedded in our memory and character when we act upon them (Bosch 1976).

From the cultivation of the vineyard of our lives we then turn to:

The Conservation of the Vineyard in Our Lives

In the parable of Jehovah's vineyard, the prophet is made to say, "My Well-beloved has a vineyard on a very fruitful hill. He dug it up and cleared out its stones, and planted it with the choicest vine. He built a tower in its midst, and also made a winepress in it; so He expected it to bring forth good grapes, but it brought forth wild grapes" (Is. 5:2). Our Lord referred to this parable during His teaching here upon earth (Matt. 21:33–46; Mark 12:1–9; Luke 20:9–19). The details, both in Isaiah and in the gospel, are virtually identical. And what the

Holy Spirit is saying to us in these words is that in order to conserve the vine and the fruit, the husbandman must gather the stones for a threefold purpose.

1. The stones must be gathered for the wall of protection. "My Well-beloved has a vineyard. . . . He dug it up and cleared out its stones" (Is. 5:1–2). As we have seen already, "Whoever breaks through a wall will be bitten by a serpent" (Eccl. 10:8). We are told that this stone wall of protection was usually surrounded by a fence, or hedge, of shrubs. This was to act as a kind of windbreaker against the storms that threatened the young vines. Stones out of place can represent thoughtlessness, carelessness, and laziness; but stones in their rightful place can symbolize the protection of our lives. Thank God for the teaching of His Word and the leading of His Spirit which enable us to protect our lives from the attacks of the world, the flesh, and the devil. I offer no hope whatsoever to anyone who imagines that he can survive the forces of evil in our day and generation without the divinely built wall of Protection. We cannot study the Bible without observing that God has placed sanctions upon our personal, social, and national life. But when we neglect the authority of God's Word and the sufficiency of God's Spirit, *the serpent bites.* Satan attacks. Outside of the protection of Jesus Christ you have no hope whatsoever. When Satan attacks, remember he is supernatural and you are only natural. You must know the mighty indwelling of the Son of God who was manifested to disintegrate the works of the devil (1 John 3:8).

2. The stones must be gathered for the watchtower of perception. "[Clear] out its stones, and . . . [build] a tower in its midst" (Is. 5:2). In order to spot unwelcome intruders, one or more towers were built in the vineyard. From these lookout points, vigilant eyes were ever surveying the landscape.

What a message this has for you and me! Jesus told His disciples that they were to "watch and pray" (Matt. 26:41). And Paul, in his Epistle to the Ephesians, exhorts his readers to "[pray] always with all prayer and supplication in the Spirit, being watchful to this end with all perseverance and supplication for all the saints" (Eph. 6:18). Watching *sights* the enemy, whereas praying *fights* the enemy. By the indwelling of the Holy Spirit and the instruction of the Holy Word, the Christian is given a kind of spiritual radar which senses the approach of evil. This is the value of the watchtower. Without it the vineyard can be ruined.

In the Song of Solomon there is a solemn word concerning the spoilers of the vineyard of our lives. The language is put in the form of this prayer, "Catch us the foxes, the little foxes that spoil the vines, for our vines have tender grapes" (Song 2:15). Very often these little foxes find a crack in the wall, and unless spotted, can enter the vineyard under cover of darkness and nibble away at the tender vines. Such destructiveness quickly spoils the promised fruitage. This is why the watchtower is so important. You and I know that it is not so much the big sins that ruin our lives, but rather the subtle little foxes that slip in through unguarded defenses to spoil the tender grapes.

But the "little foxes" are not the only cause of intrusion and destruction. The passage in Proverbs 24:33–34 is explicit here, "A little sleep, a little slumber, a little folding of the hands to rest; so shall your poverty come like a prowler, and your need like an armed man." The latter part of this verse is better rendered, "And poverty come upon you like a robber, and want like an armed man." God knows how many armed robbers constantly seek to destroy the vineyard of our lives. How important it is, then, to gather up the stones for the building of the watchtower of perception! Thank God the Word tells us, "When the enemy comes in like a flood, the Spirit of the Lord will lift up a standard against him" (Is. 59:19).

3. The stones must be gathered for the winepress of production. "My Well-beloved . . . cleared out its stones, and . . . made a winepress in it; so He expected it to bring forth good grapes" (Is. 5:1–2). We are told that stones were utilized for the construction of winepresses. Here is where the grapes were crushed in order to secure the precious wine for home use and sale.

And I have no need to tell you that this is what God wants from our lives. "The fruit of the Spirit is love, joy, peace, long-suffering, kindness, goodness, faithfulness, gentleness, self-control" (Gal. 5:22–23), and nothing less will glorify the Father. There is only one whose life pleases God, and that is Jesus Christ, His Son. And this is the only one whose life He wants reproduced in us by the Holy Spirit. The winepress speaks of the pressures and measures that He exerts upon us in order that the life of Jesus might be seen in us and through us. Anything less than this is wasted living. As He comes to your vineyard and mine, what has He to say? Are we bringing forth "fruit," "more fruit," "much fruit"? Or is the Master displeased with the lack of productivity in our lives? The only purpose in the cultivation of our lives is that there should be the conservation of fruit for His glory. We can test the success or failure of our lives on this one issue of fruitfulness.

As we have pointed out before, God says more about this matter of fruit than is commonly believed. Indeed, Jesus uttered His last word on the subject when He declared, "By this My Father is glorified, that you bear much fruit" (John 15:8). Anything less than this is falling short of the glory of God; and this by definition means a life of sin and shame.

So there is "a time to cast away stones, and a time to gather stones" (Eccl. 3:5). The one aspect concerns the cultivation of the vineyard of our lives, while the other aspect represents the conservation of the vineyard of our lives. In the light of this, ask yourself honestly and personally: Is my life a vineyard or a wilderness?

It is of striking significance that Jesus equated faith with fruit. When He saw a fig tree without the fruit He expected, He cursed it and said, "Let no one eat fruit from you ever again" (Mark 11:14). Later, when Peter recognized that the cursed fig tree had "withered away" (Mark 11:21), Jesus said to him, "Have faith in God" (Mark 11:22). The fact is, faith without fruit is dead. Have you and I a living faith? If our answer is in the affirmative, then the fruit of the Spirit will be self-evident. Jesus said that fruit is the final test of reality. Speaking of false prophets, He declared, "By their fruits you will know them" (Matt. 7:20). And this same Master comes to you and me today and asks, "Show Me your vineyard, show Me your fruit; yes, show Me your **faith,**" for "without faith it is impossible to please [God]" (Heb. 11:6).

I mentioned earlier that the only One who always pleased the Father was the Lord Jesus Christ. It follows, therefore, that if we would please God, we must allow the Lord Jesus to live out His life in us day by day. So I ask you, as I ask myself, Is Jesus revealed in you? Remember,

> What the world needs is Jesus,
> Just a glimpse of Him.

Think on These Things (Phil. 4:8)

In the early church, the followers of Jesus were conspicuous by their Christian boldness and likeness to the Christ they loved and served. It is recorded that when the rulers, elders, and scribes "saw the *boldness* of Peter and John, and perceived that they were uneducated and untrained men, they *marveled*. And they realized that they [Peter and John] had been with Jesus" (Acts 4:13). There was an unmistakable Christ-like fragrance which exuded from the garden of their lives.

9

A Time to Embrace and a Time to Refrain from Embracing

*P*rofessor Henry Drummond (1969) says that "the greatest thing in all the world is love," and Paul reminds us that among the gifts to man there are three of outstanding quality: faith, hope and love, "these three; but the greatest of these is love" (1 Cor. 13:13). It is John, however, who declares the final word when he affirms that "God is love" (1 John 4:8). In saying this, the apostle is informing us that love is more than "the greatest thing," or even the "greatest gift." Love is *God* giving and forgiving; love is not impressive verbosity, but redemptive activity.

The Bible teaches, moreover, that love not only *has* its own laws, but *keeps* its own laws. Indeed, "love is the fulfillment of the law" (Rom. 13:10). Thus Solomon establishes a principle when he says there is "a time to embrace, and a time to refrain from embracing" (Eccl. 3:5). This means that there is the constraint of love, and there is likewise the restraint of love. Let us proceed to examine these two aspects of the greatest thing in all the world.

The Constraint of Love

As we have observed, love is never static: it is always active. We have to read only the song of love as recorded in the 13th chapter of 1 Corinthians to see this. There we have set forth the priority, activity, and eternity of this greatest of all gifts. Essentially, love is fellowship between persons. It is an act of self-surrender. This is how love operates between the Father, Son, and Holy Spirit. And this is how love ought to operate among the sons of men here upon earth. So we see that there is such a thing as the embrace, or constraint, of love.

For the purpose of this study, let us begin with the constraint of *spiritual* love. The apostle John sums up the constraint of spiritual love when he says, "We love Him because he first loved us" (1 John 4:19). If we understand the nature of spiritual love, we cannot withhold an appropriate response.

The New Testament is full of examples of this quality of response. Think of the love response of *conversion* in the life of the woman who entered Simon's house to anoint the feet of her Savior and Lord (Luke 7:36–40, 50). We read that she "kissed His feet and anointed them with the fragrant oil" (Luke 7:38). Little wonder that Jesus turned to her and said: "Your faith has saved you. Go in peace" (Luke 7:50). No one who appreciates full and free forgiveness can withhold the love response of conversion.

Then we read of the love response of *communion*. Consider Mary, the sister of Lazarus, who came to the Lord Jesus on the eve of His passion with a pound of ointment of spikenard, very costly, and anointed the feet of Jesus until the house was filled with the fragrance of the precious oil. Our Savior's comment to those who criticized her was, "Let her alone; she has kept this for the day of My burial" (John 12:7). Here was a woman whose communion with the Lord Jesus had given her an understanding of His redemptive mission beyond any one of the disciples. She knew what Jesus was about to accomplish at Calvary, and in appreciation of His sacrifice, she presented her own sacrifice. Truly, this was the love response of communion.

Another telling example is the love response of *confession*. This occurred when Peter opened his heart to the Savior and cried, "Lord, You know all things; You know that I love You" (John 21:17). He had miserably denied his Lord, but having sought forgiveness and restoration, he now matched his denial of Christ by his devotion to Christ in genuine love.

This, then, is what we call the constraint of spiritual love—"We love Him because he first loved us" (1 John 4:19). There is "a time to embrace" (Eccl. 3:5).

Then there is the constraint of *social love*. Before He went back to glory the Lord Jesus said to His disciples, "This is My commandment, that you love one another as I have loved you" (John 15:12). In fact, He added, "By this all will know that you are My disciples, if you have love for one another" (John 13:35). This is the supreme evidence of true discipleship, and the rest of Scripture corroborates this.

The constraint of social love involves the *family*. Addressing the head of the household, Paul says, " Husbands, love your wives, just as Christ also loved the church and gave Himself for her" (Eph. 5:25). And just as the Lord Jesus is the Head of the whole church, so the husband is the head of the whole family. A home is no longer a home where love does not exist between husband and wife, parents and children; in this context there is "a time to embrace."

The constraint of social love involves the *brotherhood*. Peter says, "Love the brotherhood" (1 Pet. 2:17). This, of course, is another name for the community of the redeemed, or the fellowship of the church. Such was the love among the brother-hood, in the early days of the Christian church, that the pagans had to exclaim, "See how these Christians love one another." There is nothing that convinces the world of the reality and authority of the church of Christ like a manifestation of such love. Surely, it is "a time to embrace."

The constraint of social love involves the *neighbor*. Jesus said, "You shall love your neighbor as yourself" (Matt. 22:39). This is the natural overflow of our love to God. If we truly love God with all our heart, our soul, our mind, and strength, we cannot but love our neighbor as ourselves. It is because we have lost the vertical constraint of spiritual love that we fail to experience the horizontal constraint of social love. The secret of social action is not so much a matter of governmental policies or beneficial niceties, but rather a matter of spiritual power and action. In this regard, there is "a time to embrace," and the world around is waiting to see this.

The constraint of social love involves the *enemy*. The Master said, "Love your enemies, bless those who curse you, do good to those who hate you, and pray for those who spitefully use you and persecute you" (Matt. 5:44). Only Calvary can bring about this miracle of forgiving love. The Lord Jesus exhibited this social concern when He was being nailed to a wooden cross. Instead of cursing His enemies He prayed, "Father, forgive them, for they do not know what they do" (Luke 23:34). That same spirit of loving concern motivated Stephen, as he was being stoned to death, for he, like the Master, cried with a loud voice: " 'Lord, do not charge them with this sin.' And when he had said this, he fell asleep" (Acts 7:60). So even in the moment of death there is "a time to embrace."

With the constraint of social love, there is also the constraint of *sexual love*. The sanctity of sex is one of the great themes of Biblical revelation. When God created Adam and Eve, He pronounced their relationship as "very good" (Gen. 1:31). Indeed, it was He who saw that it was not good for man to be alone, and so produced a help meet for Adam. In His purpose and plan He willed that husband and wife should enjoy the constraint of sexual love.

Commenting on this aspect of love, Paul says, "Let each man have his own wife, and let each woman have her own husband" (1 Cor. 7:2). Then he adds, "Let the husband render to his wife the affection due her, and likewise also the wife to her husband" (1 Cor. 7:3). The Revised Standard Version renders this even more specifically: "The husband should give to his wife her conjugal rights, and likewise the wife to her husband." The only exception to this normal practice is a mutual restraint for the purposes of fasting and prayer. So the apostle continues, "Do not deprive one another except with consent for a time, that you may give yourselves to fasting and prayer; and come together again so that Satan does not tempt you because of your lack of self-control" (1 Cor. 7:5). Under the control of the Holy Spirit, the constraint of sexual love can be real and romantic for as long as God wills it. On the other hand, to grieve the Holy Spirit in this regard is to despise God and to merit the vengeance of the Lord (1 Thess. 4:6, 8).

So there is "a time to embrace," but there is also "a time to refrain from embracing" (Eccl. 3:5). It is:

The Restraint of Love

Someone may well ask whether there is any Scripture that forbids us from loving. The answer, of course, is in the affirmative. Writing to his converts, the apostle John says: "*Do not love* the world or the things in the world. If anyone loves the world, the love of the Father is not in him. For all that is in the world—the lust of the flesh, the lust of the eyes, and the pride of life—is not of the Father but is of the world. And the world is passing away, and the lust of it; but he who does the will of God abides forever" (1 John 2:15–17). It is quite clear from these verses that the restraint of love prohibits the lust of the flesh, the lust of the eyes, and the pride of life.

In terms of human relationships, *the restraint of love prohibits the unlawful embrace*—"the lust of the flesh" (1 John 2:16). Contrary to the tenets of the "new morality" and "situation ethics," love has its own laws. Paul makes this abundantly clear when he states, "For he who loves another has fulfilled the law" and then immediately adds, "You shall not commit adultery. . . . Love does no harm to a neighbor; therefore love is the fulfillment of the law" (Rom. 13:8–10). The biblical interpretation of love is seen only within the context of God's moral law; therefore, there is such a thing as the *unlawful* embrace. Indeed, the Scriptures are very clear on this. For example—Paul advises, "It is good for a man *not* to touch a woman" (1 Cor. 7:1). That word "touch" is an important one. Our Authorized Version tends to mislead us. Actually the verb means, "to fasten to," "to kindle a fire," or "to handle with intention." Without question, it has reference to the unlawful embrace.

Now in this age of permissiveness, such an apostolic prohibition is simply scoffed at, but this does not alter the clear teaching of the Word of God. The Bible says:

> For this is the will of God, your sanctification: that you should abstain from sexual immorality; that each of you should know how to possess his own vessel in sanctification and honor, not in passion of lust, like the Gentiles who do not know God; *that no one should take advantage of and defraud his brother in this matter, because the Lord is the avenger of all such, as we also forewarned you and testified.* For God did not call us to uncleanness, but in holiness. Therefore he who rejects this does not reject man, but God, who has also given us His Holy Spirit. (1 Thess. 4:3–8)

The Christian has no business to defraud or overreach in the matter of sexual appeal and activity. To persist in such a course of action is to merit the judgment of God. The Bible says, "The Lord is the avenger of all such, as we also forewarned you" (1 Thess. 4:6), and again, "Marriage is honorable among all, and the bed undefiled; but fornicators and adulterers God will judge" (Heb. 13:4). If I understand my Bible, this cuts out sexual petting, necking, and intercourse—outside of the lawful bounds of marriage.

We note further that in human relationships *the restraint of love prohibits the unrealistic* embrace—"the lust of the eyes" (1 John 2:16). When a person fears the consequences of the unlawful embrace, he resorts to the realm of the pornographic. Through the eye gate he creates the unrealistic world of imaginative happenings—with all their lustful consequences.

Now the Lord Jesus severely dealt with this kind of situation. He declared:, "Whoever looks at a woman to lust for her has already committed adultery with her in his heart" (Matt. 5:28)—which simply implies that sin within the realm of the imagination is just as serious before God as sin in the realm of physical involvement. The modern pornographic literature, the nudity plays, and the movies on sexual intercourse are evidence of a corrupt and corrupting society. As Christian people, we should protest such things, not only by nonparticipation, but also by the restraint of our love.

Still another factor in this matter of human relationships is *that the restraint of love prohibits the unspiritual embrace*—"the pride of life" (1 John 2:16). Pride and vainglory are the very antithesis of spirituality. And in no area is unspirituality more common than in the matter of love, courtship, and marriage. The fact is that carnal people do not want God to interfere with their love affairs. And yet no one can read the Bible without observing that God has a plan for every life, and within that plan is His purpose for love, courtship, and marriage. This is why the Lord Jesus referred His disciples to the early chapters of Genesis for the final word on this subject. To study these verses is to discover that God has a pattern for those who want His *best*.

There is, first of all, God's *concern* in the matter of love, courtship, and marriage. It was He who said, "It is not good that man should be alone; I will make him a helper comparable to him" (Gen. 2:18). Adam had never seen a woman, nor would he have been able to analyze what was missing in his life. And so God revealed this to him. Surely the lesson is obvious. God knows better than we do whether or not we need a partner, and who that partner might be. Only a proud person would rebel against this concern of God.

There is, secondly, God's *control* in the matter of love, courtship, and marriage. We read that "the Lord God caused a deep sleep to fall on Adam, and he slept; and He took one of his ribs, and closed up the flesh in its place. Then the rib which the Lord God had taken from man He made into a woman" (Gen. 2:21–22). Adam's willingness to sleep in the will of God shows his faith in the divine preparation and revelation of a true helpmeet. Anything less than this would have been "the pride of life" (1 John 2:16). Again, the lesson is obvious. If we desire God's choice for us, then we must submit to God's control over us. To refuse this divine control is an evidence of pride and unbelief.

Thirdly, there is God's *consummation* in the matter of love, courtship, and marriage. The Record informs us that "the Lord God . . . brought her to the man" (Gen. 2:22). Because this was God's choice, it proved to be a perfect match. There was an affinity of spirit, for "the Lord God . . . brought her to the man" (Gen. 2:22). Adam and Eve met in God. There was no unequal yoke. Then, further, there was an affinity of soul. Adam said, "She shall be called Woman, because she was taken out of man" (Gen. 2:23). As a woman, she was the complement of the man, and therefore, in every sense, an "helpmeet." Here is the answer to the incompatibilities of mind, heart, and will which ruin so many marriages. There was also an affinity of body. Adam said, "This is now bone of my bones and flesh of my flesh" (Gen. 2:23). Physically, she was just right for Adam. This would satisfy such important considerations as age, size, and health. God never makes mistakes in marriages.

So when He brings two lives together there is perfect consummation.

Now the question arises as to man's response to God's plan for human life. If he is spiritual he will want nothing but God's way. On the other hand, if he is carnal he will want man's way. This is why our society today is organized to swell our pride, build our egos, and insist on our rights when it comes to finding a wife or husband. Father and mother interfere, friends exert pressure, and Madison Avenue and Hollywood condition the outlook. But the Bible, with unchanging authority, declares, "There is . . . a time to refrain from embracing" (Eccl. 3:1, 5), and such restraint of love prohibits the unspiritual embrace.

So we have seen what God has to say on "the greatest thing in all the world." The issues are clear. We can choose man's way or God's way. To choose God's way is to know fulfillment and contentment; to choose man's way is to experience frustration and ultimate failure. Are you prepared to choose God's way when it comes to this matter of love, courtship, and marriage? Do you think God is interested? I've talked about God's concern, God's control, and God's consummation in this matter. It is the number one priority in the purpose of God for your life. Anything less than that is a huge mistake. If you can trust the Heavenly Father for such little details as your shopping list and your daily activities, why shouldn't you trust Him for the most important thing in your life outside of conversion? Are you prepared to act upon these principles and let Him do the choosing? God's will is "good, pleasing and perfect" (Rom. 12:2, NIV).

Think on These Things (Phil. 4:8)

Second only to the creation of Adam was God's plan for a "helpmeet" for him. In a similar sense, next to our new creation in Christ is God's plan for an "helpmeet" for those of us who are destined to be married "in the Lord." The solemn question we must answer is clear: Is it "time to embrace" or "to refrain from embracing?" It is significant that this word "embrace," which occurs some twelve times in the Old Testament, is used in three specific ways: The first use of the term expresses the idea of embracing someone else to show fondness or affection (Gen. 29:13; 48:10; 2 Kgs. 4:16; Job 24:8). The second use of the word describes the embrace of lovers. This embrace can designate virtuous love (Song 2:6) or the adulterous embrace of a wrong relationship (Prov. 6:27, 32–33). The third idea of "folding of hands" is an implicit designation of self-love (Prov. 6:10; 24:33). Each one of us must *choose* God's will or our self-will.

10

A Time to Gain
and a Time to Lose

You have heard it said, "It is the decisions that kill me"; and there is an element of truth in that. It all depends on the kind of decisions that are made. If we make the right choices, the inevitable consequences will be demonstrated in a life of righteousness. On the other hand, if we make the wrong choices, the effects will be manifested in a life of sinfulness. It is not easy to make the unpopular decision. In the book of Esther, we read that Queen Vashti refused to parade her beauty before a company of drunken and lustful men, and as a result, she lost her position of favor before the king. But she kept her moral integrity. We also have to decide between popularity and integrity. If we choose the latter we may be laughed at by the crowd, but we will retain something far more important—our honor.

Sooner or later there comes a time in human experience when a person has to decide on his or her life's ambition. Is it to be earthly gain or heavenly gain? Is the object of existence to be the service of self or the worship of God? Such a momentous decision involves the exercise of personal choice. And this is precisely what the Preacher has in mind when he says, "There is . . . a time to gain, and a time to lose" (Eccl. 3:1, 6). Literally, the Hebrew reads, "To seek has its time, and to lose has its time." So the Holy Spirit would have us understand that somewhere along our earthly journey we have to seek, if we are to find, and we have to lose if we are to gain. To interpret these concepts we must observe that:

There Is a Time to Choose God's Purpose for Life

To "gain" or to "seek" presupposes the right of choice. This principle applies in every area of life. If a person decides to make his ambition that of wealth, fame, or power, he has made a choice. By the same token, if he determines to set his affection on things above, he likewise has made a choice. At some point in human experience there must be a time to choose. This solemn fact inevitably brings us to consider *the sovereignty of choice.*

When God created man, He endowed him with life's greatest gift: power of choice. And within the beauties and duties of the Garden of Eden, Adam was given the freedom to exercise his right of choice, even though this involved the possibility of disobeying the will of God. This is why his Creator said to him, "Of every tree of the garden you may freely eat; but of the tree of the knowledge of good and evil you shall not eat, for in the day that you eat of it you shall surely die" (Gen. 2:16–17). Not to have allowed this sovereignty of choice would have made Adam nothing more than a robot. We know, of course, that when put to the test, Adam misused his sovereignty of choice and through disobedience brought sin into the world, and death by sin (Rom. 5:12). The apostle Paul tells us that when offered the forbidden fruit "Adam was *not* deceived" (1 Tim. 2:14). This means that with the full knowledge of the consequences, he transgressed the will of his Creator. In like manner, we can choose whether or not we please ourselves, or "seek first the kingdom of God and *his* righteousness" (Matt. 6:33). You and I have the power of sovereign choice.

But more than this, we must recognize *the urgency of choice*. This was the burden of Joshua's final message to the children of Israel. Addressing them on that historic occasion he said, "Choose for yourselves *this day* whom you will serve. . . . But as for me and my house, we will serve the Lord" (Josh. 24:15). His emphasis was on the urgency of making the right choice.

And this note of urgency is found again and again throughout the Scriptures. Paul sums up the matter when he says, "Behold, *now* is the accepted time; behold, now is the day of salvation" (2 Cor. 6:2). Life, at best, is so short, and yet what wasted moments, hours, days, and years we shall have to lament when we stand before the judgment throne! We tend to forget that everyone will have to give account of himself. Not only will our works be evaluated, but our very words. Jesus made this plain when He cautioned, "Every idle word men may speak, they will give account of it in the day of judgment" (Matt. 12:36).

Thus we see that there is such a thing as the urgency of choice. This is why the devil concentrates every effort to make us procrastinate.

Someone once had a dream in which he found himself in hell, overhearing a discussion between Satan and his demons. "But what is the method for keeping people from entering the kingdom of our Enemy?" asked Satan.

"Disprove the existence of God," suggested one demon.

"But that is no use," replied Satan. "At no time in history has man been able to accept atheism. There is a fundamental God-consciousness in him that no amount of argument or debate can change. The fact that there are so few individuals who call themselves atheists only goes to prove my point."

"Well, let us try to undermine faith in the Bible," urged another demon. "That is no use either," countered the devil. "Think back through the centuries and recall what has been done to destroy this Book. It has been attacked by the greatest minds, it has been banned, and even burned, but from the ashes of such burnings have sprung up even more translations and also the men and women to proclaim its message. No, undermining faith in the Bible will not do."

"Then I have an idea," blurted out a more thoughtful demon. "Let us start a campaign to spread the idea that there is plenty of time and, therefore, there is no hurry or urgency to consider spiritual things."

"That's it!" exclaimed Satan, "You could not be more accurate or relevant. Men and women, by virtue of their natures, will fall for that proposition; and, of course, it is fatal, as far as their eternal destiny is concerned. But why should I care, as long as they finish up in hell?"

With the urgency of choice, there is also the *destiny* of choice. In this regard, we need to think of a man like Moses. We read in Hebrews 11:24–27 that:

> by faith Moses, when he became of age, refused to be called the son of Pharaoh's daughter, choosing rather to suffer affliction with the people of God than to enjoy the passing pleasures of sin, esteeming the reproach of Christ greater riches than the treasures in Egypt; for he looked to the reward. By faith he forsook Egypt, not fearing the wrath of the king; for he endured as seeing Him who is invisible.

We cannot study these verses without being amazed at this man's sense of values. Moses, under the providence of God, had been brought up in the luxury of the Egyptian court and trained in all the learning of the Egyptian universities. If anyone had a chance to acquire earthly wealth, power, fame, and glory, it was Moses. And yet we read that he "refused to be called the son of Pharaoh's daughter, choosing rather to suffer affliction with the people of God than to enjoy the passing pleasures of sin" (Heb. 11:24–27). He weighed up the issues, he evaluated the gains and the losses, and he made a choice. The only explanation for this amazing choice is the ultimate end he had in view. Three words help us to sum it up.

There was, first of all, the *reproach* of Christ. Like Abraham, Moses rejoiced to see the day of Christ and was glad. What others would have considered as something to be shunned at all costs, he esteemed as a prize to be eagerly sought. With Paul, he could say that he counted "all things loss for the excellence of the knowledge of Christ Jesus [the] Lord" (Phil. 3:8). So he esteemed the reproach of Christ greater riches than the treasure of Egypt.

But then he saw something else. Beyond the glitter of the pleasure and treasures of Egypt, "he looked to the reward" (Heb. 11:26). There was the *reward* of Christ. Like the apostle, he pressed "toward the goal for the prize of the upward call of God in Christ Jesus" (Phil. 3:14). He could see beyond earthly gain to that heavenly reward.

But, supremely, Moses had eyes to perceive the *reality* of Christ, for "he endured as seeing Him who is invisible" (Heb. 11:27). To him, this was life's greatest ambition. And, of course, this was true of Paul the apostle. At the very end of his life he could say, "That I may know Him and the power of His resurrection, and the fellowship of His sufferings, being conformed to His death" (Phil. 3:10).

How this glimpse into the life of Moses shames our modern generation with its shallow outlook and materialistic ambitions! Only a man with a sense of destiny can choose the reproach of Christ, the reward of Christ, and the reality of Christ! All the men whom God has chosen to bless in this sin-cursed world of ours have been men who have chosen to forsake all for the reproach, reward, and reality of Christ. We could name such personalities as Martin Luther and his Protestant Reformation, William Carey and his modern missionary movement, David Livingstone and his vision and burden for Africa, and Roger Williams and his passion and program for religious liberty. These men "endured as seeing him who is invisible" (Heb. 11:27). There is a time, then, to choose; and we must face this choice. Will we use the sovereignty, urgency, and destiny of choice to make the right choice?

Then we must acknowledge that:

There Is a Time to Lose Man's Purpose for Life

We cannot choose *God's* purpose for life without losing *man's* purpose for life. Jesus emphasized this when He said: "Whoever desires to come after Me, let him deny himself, and take up his cross, and follow Me. For whoever desires to save his life will lose it, but whoever loses his life for My sake and the gospel's will save it" (Mark 8:34–35). Jesus specifically taught that to choose God's purpose for life involves losing our own life for the sake of the gospel.

Someone might object, "But to lose one's life in Christ is to lose individuality." We reply that nothing could be further from the truth. To lose our lives in Christ is to find complete individuality, for only in Christ is the human personality truly totalized (Col. 2:10).

This loss of our lives in Christ means that we must *deny for Christ*—"If anyone desires to come after Me, let him deny himself" (Luke 9:23). This calls for the renunciation of anything and everything in our lives that would hinder the fulfillment of God's purposes.

I love that dramatic touch of Mark when he tells the story of blind Bartimeus (Mark 10:46–52). The opportunity of a lifetime had come, for Jesus had bidden the beggar to come to Him for healing. And we read that "throwing aside his garment, he rose and came to Jesus" (Mark 10:50). There was nothing intrinsically wrong with that garment. On many a cold day it had kept the blind man warm, but at this point in his life it could have tripped him in coming to Christ, so he cast it aside. Indeed, he sacrificed the good for the better, and the better for the best. Nothing was going to impede his advance to the only One who could heal him and save him.

Are you and I prepared to do this? Are we prepared to cast away anything that would hold us back from experiencing God's highest purpose for our lives? For some, this may involve the initial step of salvation; for others, this may be a new surrender to the sovereignty of Jesus Christ; for still others, this may signify the claiming of the fullness of the Holy Spirit. Whatever it is, however, you and I have to lose before *we gain*; we must deny for Christ.

The figure drawn for us in the 12th chapter of Hebrews is that of a long-distance runner. Commenting on this passage, Dr. M. R. DeHaan says:

> Some things which may not be evil in themselves still hinder us in the service of Christ. They may be just little habits or indulgences which have no spiritual value, like wasting our time in reading "empty" literature, excessive participation in sports, or preoccupation with social activities. If these things cut into our prayer life, Bible study, or Christian service, they are wrong! (Bosch 1975)

The believer must go forward unhampered by the things of the world willingly sacrificing even legitimate pleasures, if necessary, to gain the prize of God's special approval at the end of life's race (see 1 Cor. 9:24, 25).

Alexander Maclaren, that great preacher and theologian of the 19th century, said, "If we would run well on the Christian pathway, *we must run light*! To do that, we must constantly look to Jesus and not allow even so-called 'good things' to hinder us as we go forward for God."

But then, again, we must *decide for Christ*—"If anyone desires to come after Me, let him deny himself, and take up his cross daily, and follow Me" (Luke 9:23). Deciding for Christ involves both a relationship and discipleship. The *relationship* is taking up the cross. Only through the blood of the cross can we know reconciliation with God. Only at the foot of the cross can we know the surrender of our lives to the sovereignty of God.

I recall Principal L. E. Maxwell of Canada telling the story of a girl from a wealthy home who was sent to a finishing school in Europe to complete her education. During one school term the girl was invited to an evangelistic service where she was gloriously saved. Being an honest girl, she wrote home at once and shared her newfound joy with her parents.

On receipt of the letter, the father cabled her to come home immediately. Obediently, she followed instructions and arrived home in a matter of hours. As the chauffeur helped her out of the Cadillac, her mother met her, and with hardly a greeting conducted her into the study where an infuriated father was waiting.

"Let us get right down to business," he began. "I have taken full cognizance of your recent letters and have completely made up my mind. I want you to understand that I have not spent all this money on your education in order for you to become involved in a religion of half-wits and feeble folk. Either you give up this nonsense and come to your senses, or you leave this house and all it represents *forever!*"

The girl bowed her head for a few moments, and then very quietly replied, "Father, please give me time to think it over." Then excusing herself, she stepped into the living room of that great mansion and closed the door. Once alone, she dropped on her knees, and looking into the face of her wonderful Lord, she prayed, "Loving Master, You have saved me and I can do nothing else than yield my all to Thee. I cannot go back. Give me the grace to face the consequences."

Rising from her knees, she went over to the piano, and sit-ting down she began to play and sing Henry F. Lyte's hymn:

> Jesus, I my cross have taken,
> All to leave and follow Thee;
> Destitute, despised, forsaken,
> Thou, from hence, my all shalt be:
> Perish every fond ambition,
> All I've sought, and hoped, and known;
> Yet how rich is my condition,
> God and heaven are still my own!

As her voice penetrated the building, the door suddenly opened and her father entered—with tears coursing down his cheeks. "My darling," he exclaimed, "forgive me, forgive me! I had no idea that Jesus Christ meant so much to you. Will you lead your wicked old father to a similar faith in your Lord and Savior?"

Deciding for Christ is taking up the cross. But it also means following Jesus. The Master said, "If anyone desires to come after Me, let him deny himself, and take up his cross daily, and follow Me" (Luke 9:23). Following Jesus is *disciple-ship*. This entails losing ourselves in a day-by-day walk with Christ, going His way—cost what it will—until the fight is won and the journey's done. Only as we lose our lives in Christ and His gospel shall we find them in all the fullness of God's redemptive purpose. And all this demands Christian discipleship.

The challenge is obvious and inescapable. Are we prepared to choose God's purpose for our lives—and perhaps even more importantly—are we prepared to *lose* man's purpose for our lives? Our decision will determine our destiny.

Think on These Things (Phil. 4:8)

It is not without significance that our last two studies have focused on the vitally important matter of *choice*. In the final analysis, we *are* what we choose. Jim Elliott, who dedicated his life to missionary service during a week of revival meetings I conducted at Wheaton College in January 1948, wrote these words before he was speared to death in his attempt to win the Aucas for Christ in the jungles of the Amazon, "He is no fool who gives what he cannot keep, to gain what he cannot lose."

11

A Time to Keep
And a Time to Throw Away

During days of inflation, there is very little chance of saving anything. With the rising costs of food, gas, and clothes—not to speak of medical and other expenses—the paycheck shrinks before we know it. All this makes us very conscious of the word "investment." If we are wise in our financial affairs we try to save, whatever the cost. While this is important in the material realm, how seldom do we think of the spiritual realm! The Bible says, "Do not lay up for yourselves treasures on earth, where moth and rust destroy and where thieves break in and steal; but lay up for yourselves treasures in heaven, where neither moth nor rust destroys and where thieves do not break in and steal. For where your treasure is, there your heart will be also" (Matt. 6:19–21).

At first glance, there seems to be very little difference between the statements, "A time to gain, and a time to lose" and "a time to keep, and a time to throw away" (Eccl. 3:6). On closer examination, however, it is evident that the first part of the verse has to do with the matter of choice, while the second part relates to the consequences of choice. When a person has chosen to walk God's way, rather than man's way, he will also take steps to invest in heavenly things and to divest himself of earthly things. Franz Delitzsch (1900, 258) captures this thought when he renders the text, "To lay up has its time, and to throw away has its time." With this in mind, it is plain to see that there is:

A Time for Heavenly Investment

One of the subtlest devices of the devil is to blind sinners and saints alike to the concept of eternity, or what D. R. Davies (1946) used to call "the world we have forgotten." On the other hand, the Scriptures exhort us to "set [our] mind[s] on things above, not on things on the earth" (Col. 3:2). As citizens of heaven, we should be thinking constantly of our heavenly investments. The New Testament, in particular, teaches that there are at least three investments that should be made in the light of eternity:

1. There must be the investment of life. "I beseech you therefore, brethren, by the mercies of God, that you present your bodies a living sacrifice, holy, acceptable to God, which is your reasonable service. And do not be conformed to this world, but be transformed by the renewing of your mind, that you may prove what is that good and acceptable and perfect will of God" (Rom. 12:1–2). The word "bodies" can be rendered "faculties," embracing spirit, soul, body, and everything else that is involved in the human personality. *Only* as these faculties are worthily and totally yielded to God can a person prove "what is that good and acceptable and perfect will of God." And, of course, *only* "he who does the will of God abides forever" (1 John 2:17). To be conformed to this world is nothing less than to love the world and all that is in it, even "the lust of the flesh, the lust of the eyes, and the pride of life" (1 John 2:16). And we are warned, "the world is passing away" (1 John 2:17). How important it is then, that our entire lives should be submitted to the will of God so that our living and serving may abide forever.

Our example in this matter of knowing and doing the will of God is our Lord Jesus Christ. He could say, "I have come to do Your will, O God" (Heb. 10:9); "My food is to do the will of Him who sent Me, and to finish His work" (John 4:34); and finally, "Not My will, but Yours, be done" (Luke 22:42). In the model prayer He taught His disciples, He inserted as the central phrase, "Your will be done on earth as it is in heaven" (Matt. 6:10).

We are obliged to recognize, therefore, that to live for the world is ultimately to lose everything, whereas to live for the will of God is to abide forever. This is the wise investment of life.

2. *There must be the investment of time.* "See then that you walk circumspectly, not as fools but as wise, redeeming the time, because the days are evil" (Eph. 5:15–16). Time is one of the most precious commodities that has been made available to mankind. Time, moreover, has been forever sanctified by the birth, life, death, and resurrection of the Lord Jesus Christ. Because He entered time He has enriched it with an eternal significance which is both creative and redemptive. With Paul we can say, "*Behold, now is the accepted time; behold, now is the day of salvation*" (2 Cor. 6:2).

For this reason no one can understand the creative and redemptive purposes of God and dare to waste time! Indeed, we shall be judged one day in relation to our use of time while here upon earth. Thus we are exhorted to redeem the time, or buy up the time; and according to the apostle, this involves living a Spirit-filled life, for following the words "redeeming the time" he says, "Be filled with the Spirit" (Eph. 5:18). How shattering to realize that moments, hours, or days lived apart from the mastership and leadership of the Spirit are totally wasted! It is imperative, then, that the Holy Spirit be received, enthroned, and obeyed. If we have never *initially* received Him, then we must "repent, and . . . be baptized in the name of Jesus Christ for the remission of sins; and . . . receive the gift of the Holy Spirit" (Acts 2:38). We must also recognize that "as many as are led by the Spirit of God, these are sons of God" (Rom. 8:14)—and enthrone the Spirit, for "where the Spirit of the Lord is, there is liberty" (2 Cor. 3:17). Only when the Spirit is enthroned as Lord can He liberate and lead in daily life. But more than this, we must *know in personal experience* that God gives "the Holy Spirit . . . to those who obey Him" (Acts 5:32). The Christian life is not an aimless journey down an unknown way, but rather a mapped out plan and pathway that we can find, follow, and finish under the guidance of the Holy Spirit. To be filled with the Spirit, therefore, is to redeem the time and invest in eternity!

3. There must be the investment of wealth. Jesus said, "Do not lay up for yourselves treasures on earth, where moth and rust destroy and where thieves break in and steal; but lay up for yourselves treasures in heaven, where neither moth nor rust destroys and where thieves do not break in and steal. For where your treasure is, there your heart will be also" (Matt. 6:19–21). There is *an earthly investment that results in ultimate wastefulness*. This is what Jesus was talking about when He said, "Do not lay up for yourselves treasures on earth." Then He went on to point out that earth is the place of moths, rust, and thieves. The connotations behind these words conveyed a tremendous challenge to the eastern mind, for wealth in those days was evaluated in terms of cloth, grain, gold, and so on. You will remember that Gehazi, the servant of Elisha, coveted "changes of garments" (2 Kgs. 5:22), and Achan lusted after "a beautiful Babylonian garment" (Josh. 7:21). Garments like these, however, were soon destroyed when moths invaded the house or tent.

Then Jesus spoke about the rust, or more accurately, the "rot that doth corrupt." Here He was thinking of the grain stored away in barns. This, likewise, was wealth until the rats, the mice, and the worms started to eat away and spoil the harvest.

Then He described the thieves who "break through [to] steal" the treasures hidden away in the home.

What a warning this is to those of us who lay up treasure here upon earth! "We brought nothing into this world, and it is certain we can carry nothing out" (1 Tim. 6:7). And even worse than this, while in the world, clothes can be antiquated, our grain can be dissipated, and our gold can be confiscated! Times may have changed, but the relative worth of earthly treasure remains the same.

On the other hand, there is a *heavenly investment that results in ultimate wealthiness*. So the Master said, "Lay up for yourselves treasures in heaven, where neither moth nor rust destroys and where thieves do not break in and steal" (Matt. 6:20). In this context Jesus had been speaking of *giving* as worthy of heavenly recompense. Concerning this giving, Jesus said, "Do not let your left hand know what your right hand is doing, that your charitable deed may be in secret; and your Father who sees in secret will Himself reward you openly" (Matt. 6:3–4). It is the disciplined and unostentatious giving, performed in the presence of God, which constitutes laying up treasure in heaven.

The Lord Jesus emphasized this again in the parable of the unjust steward, where He summed up the lesson in these words, "Make friends for yourselves by unrighteous mammon, that when you fail, they may receive you into an everlasting home" (Luke 16:9). In effect, He was saying that if you have money, you are to use it in such a way that when you get to heaven the people who have benefited from it will receive you with joy. The same truth is expressed by Paul when he exhorts: "Command those who are rich in this present age not to be haughty, nor to trust in uncertain riches but in the living

God, who gives us richly all things to enjoy. Let them do good, that they be rich in good works, ready to give, willing to share, storing up for themselves a good foundation for the time to come, that they may lay hold on eternal life" (1 Tim. 6:17–19).

Jesus concluded His teaching on heavenly investment with the words, "Where your treasure is, there your heart will be also" (Matt. 6:21; Luke 12:34). How true this is! Show me a man who is engaged in heavenly investment, and I will show you a person who is totally devoted to Jesus Christ. Paul dramatically exemplifies this when he ends his last epistle with that noble testimony: "I have fought the good fight, I have finished the race, I have kept the faith. Finally, there is laid up for me the crown of righteousness, which the Lord, the righteous Judge, will give to me on that Day, and not to me only but also to all who have *loved* His appearing" (2 Tim. 4:7–8). And then with heartache he adds, "Demas has forsaken me, having *loved* this present world" (2 Tim. 4:10). Whether we love the Lord Jesus and anticipate His coming, or we love the world and concern ourselves with its interests, one thing is certain: we can't do both at one and the same time.

Are we investing in heavenly things or in worldly things? On what are we staking our lives, our time, our wealth?

The story is told of a very wealthy Englishman who lived in a palatial home on his own estate. Among his servants he had a gardener who was a perfect saint. The life he lived and the testimony he bore were real and radiant. For some years the Englishman despised his gardener, even though he could not criticize his work. Little by little, however, the gardener's witness overcame hostility and won his master to a saving knowledge of Christ.

Soon after this the gardener became seriously ill and died. Filled with grief at the loss, this wealthy Englishman one night had a dream and found himself in heaven. He requested at once to see his old gardener, and an angel in white conducted him down the golden streets of that celestial city to an exquisite mansion.

"This," said the angel, "is the abiding place of your former gardener." The Englishman was completely overcome, but then asked, "But where will be my mansion?"

"Down this way," replied the angel, and on and on they went until they came to the most unpretentious little house at the end of a side street. "This," emphasized the angel, "is *your* place of abode."

"How can that be?" objected the man, "I have lived in a mansion when I was on earth!"

"That is precisely it," explained the angel; "your gardener was forever laying up treasure in heaven, and the mansion he possesses was built with the material that he sent up here. At the same time you laid up treasure on earth, and what little you did forward to heaven has been put to good use."

This was only a dream, but it is also a parable. Are you, am I, laying up treasure in heaven, or are we laying up treasure on earth? There is a time to lay up. All this leads us to deduce that there is:

A Time for Earthly Divestment

Just as the New Testament has much to say on heavenly investment, so it has clear teaching on what we are terming *earthly divestment*. Perhaps the most comprehensive statement on this is found in the 12th chapter of Hebrews where we read:

> Let us lay aside every weight, and the sin which so easily ensnares us, and let us run with endurance the race that is set before us, looking unto Jesus, the author and finisher of our faith, who for the joy that was set before Him endured the cross, despising the shame, and has sat down at the right hand of the throne of God. (Heb. 12:1–2)

From this we learn two things. First, *there are weights in our lives that must be cast away*. "Let us lay aside every weight"

(Heb. 12:1). The word "weight" denotes "bulk" or "mass," and therefore metaphorically stands for an encumbrance. The rich young ruler had a weight—his riches. When he was challenged to lay his weight aside he refused, and that, in turn, led to his rejection of Christ.

If there is something in this world upon which you have set your heart, that is your weight. In and of itself, it may not be wrong, but as long as it weighs you down, it has the potential for tripping you up. Whatever the weight is, it must be cast aside.

Dr. Joseph Macaulay recounts the story of a Scottish preacher by the name of William Guthrie who wrote the classic, *The Saving Interest*. He was a born sportsman; he loved the rod and the gun. After his conversion under Samuel Rutherford and the dedication of his life to God for the preaching of the gospel, Guthrie realized that the great estate to which he had become heir would be a weight to a man of his temperament. He, therefore, signed over his property with the full possession of the land to a younger brother, that he might devote himself to the work of the gospel. This did not mean that he never fished or hunted thereafter, but it did ensure that he was not encumbered with the responsibilities, as well as the temptation, of the wealth that was formerly his. As a result of this sacrifice, Alexander Whyte could say of him, "No one could hold a candle to William Guthrie for handling broken hearts and guiding anxious inquirers" (Macaulay 1948, 227–228).

I love the young man who came up to me after a meeting in Birmingham, England, and asked with transparent sincerity, "What can I give up in order to be a better follower of Jesus Christ?"

There are the weights that must be laid aside. Like an athlete running in a race, it is essential to lay aside anything that might hinder.

Secondly, *there are wrongs in our lives that must be cast away*. "Lay aside every weight, and the *sin* which so easily ensnares us" (Heb. 12:1). It is suggestive that the phrase "every sin" is literally "the sin which doth so easily beset us." Apparently it refers to the specific sin of unbelief which contrasts with the remarkable examples of faith which are found in the former chapter (Hebrews 11). The phrase "easily beset" denotes being "well surrounded" and carries the idea of a clinging garment that would trip a runner. For the Hebrew Christian to whom these words were first addressed, the sin mentioned was clearly unbelief, but for you and me it might be something else. What is the sin which persists in tripping us up?

The New Testament has three comprehensive definitions of sin, and it is good to examine them in order to decide what must be cast out of our lives, by the power of the Holy Spirit. Sin is a *disobedient act*, for "sin is lawlessness" (1 John 3:4). To transgress the clear teaching of Scripture constitutes disobedience, and in God's sight this is sin. This is why it is so important to attend on the preaching of the Word of God. To be hearers and not doers of the Word is to sin, and to sin seriously.

Sin is also *a disloyal act*—"To him who knows to do good and does not do it, to him it is sin" (James 4:17). God has called us to a life of goodness and holiness. Not to fulfill His purpose in this regard is to sin. The apostle Paul teaches us in his Epistle to the Romans that our loyalty to God must be that of a subject to a king, of a servant to a master, and of a wife to a husband (Rom. 6:12—7:6). Anything less than this is disloyalty, and therefore sin.

But once again, sin is a *doubtful act*, "Whatever is not from faith is sin" (Rom. 14:23). Where there is no clear revelation on a certain matter there must be patient waiting upon God and further research into His Word. To act impulsively or carelessly, especially when in doubt, is to sin. The fact of the matter is, "Without faith it is impossible to please [God]" (Heb. 11:6). In the light of such teaching, let us ask ourselves again, What sin so easily entraps us? Whatever it is, it must be laid aside. Now you and I cannot do this in our own strength. Only the

Spirit of life in Christ Jesus can make us "free from the law of sin and death" (Rom. 8:2). But thank God, through faith in the Christ who died for us and rose again, we can know the releasing power of the Spirit over every weight and every wrong.

There is "a time to cast away." Let us make sure that we divest ourselves of all earthly hindrances in order that we shall "run with endurance the race that is set before us, looking unto Jesus, the author and finisher of our faith" (Heb. 12:1–2). What a challenge this presents to our modern generation. With all the secularism of a technological age we are tempted to live as if there were no world beyond our own. We forget that we are creatures of eternity and very soon will have to face death and the judgment to come. With this in mind, we need to prepare for our departure by heavenly investments and earthly divestments. God enable us to see to it that we take time to lay up that which is eternal and cast away that which is ephemeral, for the Holy Book says, "The world is passing away, and the lust of it; but he who does the will of God abides forever" (1 John 2:17).

It is not without significance that the famous American evangelist, D.L. Moody, often quoted this verse. No wonder he died exclaiming, "Earth recedes, heaven opens before me" (Pollock 1963, 317). Here is the testimony of a man who held loosely the things of this world that he might gain the things of the world to come.

Can you look into the face of the Lord Jesus and say, "I count all things but loss that I may win Christ and be found in him"? (See Phil. 3:8, 9.)

Think on These Things (Phil. 4:8)

In the light of the truths we have considered in this chapter, I invite you to weigh up prayerfully in the presence of God the following quotes (Wirt and Beckstrom 1974, 68): "The choices of time are binding in eternity"

(Jack MacArthur). "Live near to God, and all things will appear little to you in comparison with eternal realities" (Robert Murray McCheyne). "We have all eternity to celebrate our victories, but only one short hour before sunset in which to win them" (Robert Moffat).

12

A Time to Tear
And a Time to Sew

When history is written, I believe our century will be called "the age of communication." Technology has made possible the transmission of the Word through various media. Unquestionably, one of the most powerful of these at the present time is television. Here we are concerned with pictures, fiction, and fact. All of this *properly* harnessed can help us greatly in understanding biblical concepts, for the Bible is a book of pictures. God constantly speaks through visual aids. We have dramatic stories, fascinating parables, and of course the beautiful symbolism throughout the Old and New Testaments. This has been obvious as we have worked our way through Ecclesiastes 3:1–8, and will become particularly evident as we consider the words, "There is . . . a time to tear, and a time to sew" (Eccl. 3:7).

It is generally understood that these words refer to the tearing and mending of a garment. In Bible times, the act of tearing or mending a garment had a deep significance. When used in reference to God, the figure of tearing had to do with judgment, on the one hand, or salvation on the other. In relation to man, it symbolized bereavement, chastisement, and repentance. In like manner, the mending of a garment had both a divine and a human connotation. And so, as we shall see, our text is not just a repetition of the exhortation "to weep, and . . . to laugh," "to mourn, and . . . to dance" (Eccl. 3:4). Rather, it has a message of its own to sinner and saint alike.

The Time to Tear

In the Old Testament, there are at least seven words that are translated by the word "tear." Of these seven, the particular word in this text occurs no almost sixty times. To expound each one in its context would be quite a study! However, a general idea runs right through each mention of the word "tear," whether in the Old or New Testaments.

We discover, for instance, that there is *a tearing which is divine*. As paradoxical as it may seem, God tears in judgment as well as in His acts of mercy. His tearing in judgment is illustrated again and again in the Old Testament. Perhaps the most familiar example is that of King Saul, the son of Kish (1 Sam. 15:22–28). You will remember that even though Saul was the choice of the people, God, in His goodness, approved of the man—provided he obeyed the mandates of heaven. When Saul was put to the test, however, he failed miserably. Instead of fulfilling the commandment of the Lord he "feared the people and *obeyed their voice*." So Samuel had to remind him that "to obey [God] is better than sacrifice, and to heed than the fat of rams." And then he added: "Because you have rejected the word of the Lord, He also has rejected you from being king. . . . The Lord has *torn* the kingdom of Israel from you today, and has given it to a neighbor of yours, who is better than you." So there is a tearing of divine judgment.

But equally true is the tearing of divine salvation. For this we move from the Old to the New Testament. Recalling the story of our Lord's passion, Matthew tells us that "behold, the veil of the temple was *torn* in two from top to bottom; and the earth quaked, and the rocks were split" (Matt. 27:51). While there is a difference in the language, the idea of tearing is identical. Matthew is telling us here that when Jesus died on Calvary's cross, the veil of the temple was torn, and the rocks of the earth were torn. These two "tearings" gloriously set forth the redeeming character of Christ's death and resurrection. When Jesus cried, "It is finished!" (John 19:30), He fulfilled all the types and shadows of the Old Testament and met all the demands of God's holy law. So the veil of the temple was torn from top to bottom. Henceforth, the way into the holiest was made available for everyone who would come to Jesus Christ, the "one Mediator between God and men" (1 Tim. 2:5). We are thus bidden to come boldly into the holiest "by a new and living way which He consecrated for us, through the veil, that is, His flesh" (Heb. 10:20). Through the tearing of that veil we now may know that Jesus is "the way, the truth, and the life. No one comes to the Father except through [Him]" (John 14:6).

At the same time, the tearing of the rocks dramatizes the triumphant resurrection of our Lord Jesus Christ; for just as the graves were opened on that occasion, so the tomb of our Savior was opened three days later to show that He had risen from the dead to be our justifying, sanctifying, and glorifying Lord and Life.

So we see that there is "a time to tear," and when redemption's moment came, God acted in saving grace and power.

But we must also understand that there is *a tearing which is human*. While the significance of this tearing might be multiplied, there are three clear interpretations that apply to people of all times and places. There is the tearing of *bereavement*.

When Reuben returned to the pit and found that his wicked brothers had removed Joseph and sold him to the Ishmaelites, we read that in grief "he *tore* his clothes" (Gen. 37:29). And later, when the father Jacob was informed of the fate of his beloved Joseph, we are told that he "*tore* his clothes, put sackcloth on his waist, and mourned for his son many days" (Gen. 37:34).

David's bereavement over the death of Saul, and especially of Jonathan, made him take hold of his clothes and tear them in two, and so did all the men that were with him (2 Sam. 1:11).

So we see that there is the human tearing of bereavement. Convention and culture may have changed in our day, but we still know what it is to have our hearts torn in bereavement.

There is also the tearing of *chastisement*. Without doubt, one of holiest men who ever lived was Job. Because of this, God allowed him to be tested by the devil to prove that a man can trust God, even to the point of death. And the story relates that as one calamity after another fell upon him, "Job arose, *tore* his robe, and shaved his head; and he fell to the ground and worshiped" (Job 1:20). Here was a man who accepted the attacks of Satan as the chastening of the Lord, and instead of being bitter, *he tore his mantle and worshipped God*. Even in those early days of unfolding revelation, Job knew that "whom the Lord loves He chastens" (Heb. 12:6).

In the third place, there is the tearing of *repentance*. Think of the words of the prophet Joel as he calls for national repentance, " 'Now, therefore,' says the Lord, 'Turn to Me with all your heart, with fasting, with weeping, and with mourning.' So *tear* your heart, and not your garments; return to the Lord your God, for He is gracious and merciful, slow to anger, and of great kindness; and He relents from doing harm" (Joel 2:12–13). This is the kind of tearing which God demands of all men, irrespective of time, age, race, or creed. No one can know the salvation of God without repentance toward God and faith in our Lord

Jesus Christ. Anything less than repentance God refuses; but where there is repentance, there is forgiveness with God, that He might be feared (Ps. 130:4). How true are the words, "The sacrifices of God are a broken spirit, a broken and a contrite heart—these, O God, You will not despise" (Ps. 51:17).

There is "a time to tear." Let us make sure that we understand the divine as well as the human aspects of this tearing. What determines judgment or salvation is our willingness to tear our hearts in true penitence, faith, and obedience.

But with the time to tear there is likewise:

The Time to Mend

It is a curious thing that with the exception of one Scripture, the only other reference to sewing takes us into the Garden of Eden at the point in history where Adam and Eve disobeyed the word of God and brought upon themselves the curse of sin, death, and judgment. So in graphic terms we learn the meaning of the human, as well as the divine, aspect of sewing. Consider, first of all, *the sewing which is human*. In that famous passage in Genesis 3, we read that after their sin the eyes of Adam and Eve "were opened, and they knew that they were naked; and they sewed fig leaves together and made themselves coverings" (Gen. 3:7). This is the first recorded instance of man's attempt to remedy, by his own device, his condition of sinfulness, nakedness, and fearfulness.

It certainly was a condition of *sinfulness*. Adam and Eve had deliberately disobeyed the word of the Lord. God had clearly commanded that they should not eat of the tree of the knowledge of good and evil (Gen. 2:17), but in disobedience Adam and Eve ate of the fruit and suffered the consequences. Centuries later, Paul could write, "Just as through one man sin entered the world, and death through sin, and thus death spread to all men, because all sinned" (Rom. 5:12).

With the sinfulness there was the *nakedness*. Adam said, "I was afraid because I was naked; and I hid myself" (Gen. 3:10).

Up until then both Adam and Eve were clothed with the garments of light. The glory of God shone through their mortal bodies, but the moment they sinned they became naked. And even though they sewed aprons of fig leaves, they were still naked; and this is how it has ever been. No man is clothed before God until he is clothed with the righteousness of Christ. His attempts to try and substitute the garments of his own making are both foolish and futile.

With the sinfulness and nakedness there was also the *fearfulness*. Adam confessed, "I heard Your voice in the garden, and I was afraid because I was naked; and I hid myself" (Gen. 3:10). John reminds us: "If our heart condemns us, God is greater than our heart, and knows all things. Beloved, if our heart does not condemn us, we have confidence toward God" (1 John 3:20–21). Up until this time Adam had known God's perfect love, and "there is no fear in love; but perfect love casts out fear" (1 John 4:18). But the moment he sinned, he experienced the "fear [that] involves torment" (1 John 4:18).

And so it is with you and me. No one can be happy in the presence of God with an apron of fig leaves. And yet, people within the church, as well as outside of it, are busier than ever sewing fig leaves! By this means or that they imagine they will earn divine acceptance! But once again, nothing could be more foolish or futile. Like the guest with the wrong wedding garment, all who are not clothed in the righteousness of the Lord Jesus Christ will never appear before God in a favorable light, whether in time or in eternity (Matt. 22:11–13).

In view of this, it is both comforting and instructive to know of *the sewing which is divine*. In the third chapter of Genesis we read that "for Adam and his wife the Lord God made [sewed] tunics of skin, and clothed them" (Gen. 3:21). It is interesting to note that the verb in this verse is exactly the same for the *making* of the aprons. The only contextual difference is that in this instance it is God who supplied the covering.

There are few pictures in the Bible which set forth the doctrine of divine righteousness as this one. Consider, first of all, *the provision of the covering*. We are told that "the Lord God made tunics of skins" (Gen. 3:21). This was not something Adam thought out; on the contrary, it was wholly and solely a provision of God.

It is true that scholars, such as John Calvin, maintain that God commanded Adam to slay the animals and prepare the skins. But be that as it may, the fact remains that *the provision was of God*; the thought, the word, and the action were divine. And it is noteworthy to observe that the term "clothed" is rooted in the Hebrew idea of "atonement."

But with the provision there was *the price of the covering* — "tunics of skins" (Gen. 3:21). Before Adam and Eve could wear those coats, a life had to be sacrificed. From the very beginning, Adam learned that "without [the] shedding of blood there is no remission" (Heb. 9:22). So we see in this picture God's righteousness as set forth in the cross-work of Christ, whereas man's righteousness is set forth in the sin-stained works of his own hands. In the coat of skin, Adam was no longer naked, nor had he any occasion to hide himself.

In like manner, we can only be at rest when we know that God has clothed us. And we must never forget that the righteousness which is imputed to us involved the shedding of the precious blood of our Lord and Savior, Jesus Christ. Thus with John Elias we have to say: "Oh! the wretchedness of those without Christ! They are naked without clothing! sick without a Physician! famishing without the bread of life! guilty without righteousness! unclean without a fountain! lost without a Savior! damned without atonement" (Edward Morgan, 105).

But once again, there was *the purpose of the covering* —"the Lord . . . clothed them" (Gen. 3:21). It is generally acknowledged that the purpose of their covering was twofold. First and foremost, it set forth the only basis on which man can approach a holy God. Until he is clothed with the righteousness of the Lord Jesus he can never be at ease in the unapproachable light of God. This is why the Lord Jesus says, "I counsel you to buy from Me gold refined in the fire, that you may be rich; and white garments, that you may be clothed, that the shame of your nakedness may not be revealed" (Rev. 3:18).

In the second place, the clothing of Adam and Eve forever set the standard of deportment for human beings here upon earth. Until man is glorified at the coming again of our Lord Jesus Christ, he will be possessed of a sinful nature. Therefore, his nakedness will be something to cover and hide. And any attempt of civilized man to uncover himself is an evidence of serious degeneracy.

As far back as November 13, 1967, *Newsweek* published a cover story entitled "Anything Goes: Taboos in Twilight," which concerned itself with the remarkable explosion of sexual permissiveness in the arts and in the fabric of society itself. The story touched off an unprecedented response from thousands who were outraged by the new permissiveness of our modern day. Since that story appeared, the situation that it described and analyzed has become a matter of national concern. Today there are more erotic films, more blunt-spoken novels, more nudity on stage, and more sex appeal in advertising than ever before. This blatant permissiveness is having an unbelievable influence upon the arts, culture, and the community at large. We have superceded the day of Noah; we are now living in the day of Lot, with all that that implies.

I heard Montague Goodman, a British lawyer and preacher, once say, "When men and women display their nakedness it is a sure sign that a country is going to the devil." You will remember that when the sons of Sceva attempted to take the name of Jesus in vain, the evil spirit they were attempting to exorcise "leaped on them, overpowered them, and prevailed against them, so that they fled out of that house *naked and wounded*" (Acts 19:16). God always clothes; the devil always denudes.

This, then, is something of the inner meaning of this remarkable text. We have learned that there is a time to tear, and there is a time to sew. God has taken the initiative in tearing the veil of the temple, in making a new and living way into the holiest of all. He has torn the tomb and exalted His Son to the place of power and glory. Now He calls us to tear our hearts in repentance and submission to the Lordship of Christ. In response to this challenge there is a time to mend; but as we have been warned, aprons of sewed fig leaves will not do before a holy God. We need the garments of righteousness, which have been made for us through the sacrifice of the Son of God. Only the Savior's "sewing" has acceptance in the presence of God. Let us, then, tear our hearts in repentance toward God, and then, by His grace, mend our hearts in obedience to Jesus Christ as Lord—knowing that if with all our hearts we truly seek Him, we shall surely find Him (Jer. 29:13).

Think on These Things (Phil. 4:8)

Tearing and mending may appear to be a contradiction in human terms, but in Christ and His cross it is a concurrence. Opposites unite in His reconciling death. The psalmist expresses it in poetry when he sings: "Mercy and truth have met together; righteousness and peace have kissed" (Ps. 85:10). The same God who tears can mend.

13

A Time to Keep Silence
And a Time to Speak

Gipsy Smith's name will be familiar to the older generation. To younger ones, let me just say that he was an illustrious and powerful British evangelist. When Gipsy was first saved he became anxious for the conversion of his uncle. He was reluctant, however, to witness to him because it was not considered proper, among gypsies, for children to address their elders on the subject of religion. So the boy just prayed and waited for God to open the way.

One day his uncle noticed a hole in the lad's trousers and asked, "Rodney, how is it that you have worn out the knees of your trousers more quickly than the other boys?"

"I have worn them out praying that the Lord would make you a Christian, Uncle," he replied—and then burst into tears.

His uncle uttered not a word, but put his arm around his nephew and drew him to him. It was not very long after that that both were found bending their knees in prayer to the Savior (Bosch 1976).

You know, that simple story beautifully illuminates our text. Solomon says, "There is . . . a time to keep silence, and a time to speak." More than 75% of communication between one person and another is "talk." So speaking is a large part of living. It is true that we have heard some people described as "all talk and no action." What is often overlooked is that for many of us, doing is actually speaking. An executive is "doing" when he is issuing orders. So the importance of speech cannot be overestimated. But as we are going to see in this chapter, the disciplined man of God is someone who observes that "there is . . . a time to keep silence, and a time to speak." "If anyone does not stumble in word, he is a perfect man, able also to bridle the whole body" (James 3:2); and again, "If anyone among you thinks he is religious, and does not bridle his tongue but deceives his own heart, this one's religion is useless" (James 1:26). With such weighty words in mind, we need to think seriously about:

The Mastery of the Tongue

Oswald Chambers points out that:

> Sometimes it is cowardly to speak, and sometimes it is cowardly to keep silence. In the Bible the great test of man's character is his tongue (see James 1:26). The tongue came to its right place only within the lips of the Lord Jesus Christ, because He never spoke from . . . Himself. He who was the Wisdom of God Incarnate said, 'The words that I speak unto you, I speak not of myself . . . but from My relationship with the Father.' We are either too hasty or too slow: either we won't speak at all, or we speak too much, or we speak in the wrong mood. The thing that

makes us speak is the lust to vindicate ourselves. How different it was with our Lord "who did no sin neither was guile found in his mouth." You see, "guile has the ingredient of self-vindication in it." It is the spirit which makes you say, "I'll make him smart for saying that about me!" [but] that spirit was never [found] in Jesus Christ. (27)

One of the greatest achievements of Christian discipline is to know when to keep silent and when to speak, and this involves *the power of controlled speech*. This power is not found in ourselves. This is why the Bible speaks of the tongue as an untamed member. Beasts, birds, and reptiles can be tamed, but not the tongue. Indeed, the Scriptures state categorically that "no man can tame the tongue" (James 3:8). It goes without saying, then, that the power of controlled speech mustbe supernatural; and thank God, the Christian can know the secret. When Jesus Christ is Lord of our lives, He can control our tongues by first of all controlling our thoughts and tempers.

The apostle Paul speaks of controlled thoughts when he says, "For the weapons of our warfare are not carnal but mighty in God for pulling down strongholds, casting down arguments and every high thing that exalts itself against the knowledge of God, *bringing every thought into captivity to the obedience of Christ*" (2 Cor. 10:4–5). This means, of course, that Jesus must have sovereign control of all that feeds our thought life—what we inculcate in terms of reading and watching, and what we contemplate in terms of speaking and acting.

But the Lord Jesus must also have sovereign control of our tempers. Thoughts out of control are usually fired by undisciplined tempers. But thank God, there is an answer to this problem. When Christ is crowned as undisputed Lord, the Holy Spirit fills our lives, and the Bible tells us that "the fruit of the Spirit is . . . self-control" (Gal. 5:22–23).

I can testify to this power of controlled speech after many years in the Christian ministry. Time and again, I could have erupted like a volcano, but warned of this imminent danger by the inward radar of the Holy Spirit, I have claimed the self-control of the Spirit—to the glory of God and the good of my fellow man. So once again I affirm that there is a power of controlled speech; but, day by day, we need to pray, "Set a guard, O Lord, over my mouth; keep watch over the door of my lips" (Ps. 141:3).

But this leads us to examine *the purpose of controlled speech*. A moment of reflection will convince any thoughtful person that there are times in life when "silence is golden." Indeed, speaking for myself, I can say without reservation that some of the most precious experiences of my life have been times when external voices have been stilled by "the silence of eternity, interpreted by love."

Paul S. Rees writes (1963, 23): "Let no man think [that silence is] useless! Give it a larger and more meaningful place in your soul."

As I see it, there is a twofold purpose in silence. There is *the reverential silence that we must preserve*. God says, "Be still, and know that I am God" (Ps. 46:10). And Habakkuk reminds us, "The Lord is in His holy temple. Let all the earth keep silence before Him" (Hab. 2:20).

In this connection, Dr. Rees (1963, 23) says that silence is "an aid to *memory*. When we are still, the past comes back to haunt, perhaps to humble, or to make us happy." David says: "Be angry, and do not sin. Meditate within your heart on your bed, and be still" (Ps. 4:4). The Psalmist here "looks back on troubles at the time seemingly unbearable, but troubles that have left him a bigger man, with a richer soul and a finer faith. Yes, silence is the setting in which memory has its best chance, and does its noblest work" (Rees 1963, 23). But again, silence is:

a response to *mystery*. Before any mystery [we are to] "stand in awe, and sin not." Among the mysteries [we should] consider the holiness of God. Do we stand in awe of his holiness? "As he who has called you is holy," cries Peter, "so be ye holy in all matters of conduct" [1 Pet. 1:15]. There is a hushed response that should be evoked by the unsullied holiness that our poor eyes behold in God. This response is a part of worship, of penitence, of sensitive discipleship. In the presence of such mysteries how [we need] to be silent! When no other response is ready, "in silence reflect." (Rees 1963, 23)

Samuel Chadwick (1934, 25) once said, "The soul needs its silent spaces." In the rough and tumble of our noisy world, we need to welcome reverential silence to perfect "holiness in the fear of God" (2 Cor. 7:1). I know this conflicts with the flippant testimonies, empty songs, and sloppy behavior that prevails in the religious world of our day, but we have only to reflect upon the life of our wonderful Lord to see heaven's pattern of reverence and godly fear.

But, then again, there is *the preferential silence that we must observe*. Reverential silence is our response to supernatural encounters, whereas preferential silence is our response to situational encounters. No one can read the Scriptures, with any sense of discernment, without noting that there are situations in the church, in the home, and in the world where we need to be silent.

There are times in the church when we need to be silent. Solomon says, "Walk prudently when you go to the house of God; and draw near to hear rather than to give the sacrifice of fools, for they do not know that they do evil. Do not be rash with your mouth, and let not your heart utter anything hastily before God. For God is in heaven, and you on earth; therefore let your words be few" (Eccl. 5:1–2). No doubt James had these words in mind when he exhorted his readers to be "swift to hear, slow to speak, slow to wrath" (James 1:19).

We are living in a day of emphasized publicity in matters religious. Young and old alike are pressured to express themselves and to do their own thing. Not all of this is bad, but much of it can lead to "the sacrifice of fools." Before we know it, we have been rash with our mouths and have committed ourselves to vows that we do not intend to keep. All this points out the need to exercise restraint until we have truly counted the cost and claimed the power to go through with the demands of discipleship.

Then there are times in the home when we need to be silent. We have all lived long enough to know that often relationships that are *strained* call for silence. The Bible says, "A soft answer turns away wrath, but a harsh word stirs up anger" (Prov. 15:1). Alas, without God, without Christ, and without hope in the world, many a home has witnessed tragedy because of the violation of this biblical counsel. Angry words have led to flying bullets or to inevitable divorce. It is amazing how a "gentle" answer can cool the tempers, clarify the thoughts, and restore common sense. Paul tells us that "a servant of the Lord must not quarrel but be gentle to all" (2 Tim. 2:24).

Relationships that are *sad* call for silence. When Job passed through his valley of sorrow we read that his friends "sat down with him on the ground seven days and seven nights, and no one spoke a word to him, for they saw that his grief was very great" (Job 2:13). As a pastor, I can identify with this. Often I have gone to a funeral parlor, or a home, to face friends or relatives to whom grief has recently come. At such times, words—however well expressed—would mean very little. The clasp of the hand, the look in the eyes, and the divine vibrations of healing silence more adequately conveyed the comfort and consolation in moments like these.

Again, relationships that are *sweet* call for silence. I love those words in the Song of Solomon where the young maiden reveals that she sat under the shadow of her beloved "with great delight, and his fruit was sweet to [her] taste" (Song 2:3).

This is the pinnacle of true friendship. When love reaches its consummation, silence is golden because of a mutual understanding that is more eloquent than words.

My wife and I have often sat watching a glorious sunset on a summer's evening in silent communion. We have sat before a crackling fire on a wintry night without a single word, and yet in rapturous fellowship. We have sat alongside of each other driving through the country, hour after hour, enjoying one another's presence without wasting a moment on needless verbosity.

There are times in the world when we need to be silent. When our Lord was arraigned before Pontius Pilate we read that "He answered him not one word, so that the governor marveled greatly" (Matt. 27:14). And yet when Paul comments on this very incident he says, "Christ Jesus who witnessed the good confession before Pontius Pilate" (1 Tim. 6:13). There are times when *silence is a good confession.* For our Lord to have spoken on this occasion would have been self-vindication, so he remained silent. When questioned concerning his kingship, however, He was at once articulate and declared that for this reason He had come into the world, to bear witness to the truth (John 18:37). But when His accusers attacked Him personally, He chose to be silent. This is a pattern for those of us who follow in the Master's footsteps. Peter says,

> For to this you were called, because Christ also suffered for us, leaving us an example, that you should follow His steps: "Who committed no sin, nor was deceit found in His mouth"; who, when He was reviled, did not revile in return; when He suffered, He did not threaten, but committed Himself to Him who judges righteously (1 Pet. 2:21–23).

Self-vindication calls for silence.

Self-depreciation also calls for silence. There are times when to speak would be casting pearls before swine (Matt. 7:6).

David could say, "I will guard my ways, lest I sin with my tongue; I will restrain my mouth with a muzzle, while the wicked are before me" (Ps. 39:1).

I can recall occasions when to have opened my mouth in defense of the gospel would have done more harm than good. The people concerned were so drunk or irresponsible that the mention of Jesus would have elicited nothing but blasphemy and abuse. I am sure this is why Peter gives that great word on Christian witness when he writes: "Sanctify the Lord God in your hearts, and always be ready to give a defense to everyone who asks you a reason for the hope that is in you, with meekness and fear; having a good conscience, that when they defame you as evildoers, those who revile your good conduct in Christ may be ashamed" (1 Pet. 3:15–16).

There is "a time to keep silence!" But there is also "a time to speak."

The Ministry of the Tongue

Professor R. V. G. Tasker calls attention to the fact that:

> History affords numerous illustrations of the power of great oratory to encourage the depressed, to rouse the careless, to stir men and women to noble action, and to give expression to the deeper human emotions. The magic of words has played an incalculable part in the long [history] of human endeavor and human suffering" (1956, 74–75).

This is why Solomon says, "Death and life are in the power of the tongue" (Prov. 18:21). So quite simply, the ministry of the tongue is twofold. There is *the ministry of death*. In the Epistle of James there is a full chapter on the power and potential of the tongue (3:1–18). We are told how the tongue can harm life.

It is likened to a *fire*; and you and I know what devastation a fire can work, for "how great a forest a little fire kindles!"

(James 3:5). Just like the fire, the tongue can be equally destructive.

It is likened to a *beast*—and what a beast the tongue can be, in more senses than one! Man has been able to tame mammals, birds, and reptiles but has never been able to tame his tongue; for as we have seen already, "No man can tame the tongue" (James 3:8). Consequently, the tongue can effect unspeakable damage. The tongue that was given to man by his Maker, in order to communicate truth and enjoy fellowship, has become the means by which he so often deceives his fellow and dishonors his God.

It is further likened to *poison*. In fact, it is called "a deadly poison" (James 3:8). With it man can curse, and swear, and even slay. God alone knows how many lives have been poisoned and destroyed through the power of the tongue. How solemnizing it is to know that you and I are capable of such destructive power—and yet in so many instances this is the influence of the tongue in our world today. No wonder the Lord Jesus said, "Every idle word men may speak, they will give account of it in the day of judgment" (Matt. 12:36).

Thank God, however, there is another aspect of the power of the tongue. There is *the ministry of life*. In that same third chapter of James we are told that the tongue can guide people. It is likened to the *bit*, and just as the bridle controls and directs a horse, so words rightly spoken, in the power of the Holy Spirit, can guide and gladden human lives.

This is further strengthened when James goes on to speak of the tongue as a *helm*, or rudder, which steers a ship through troubled seas. How often a word fitly spoken has enabled our fellow man to see his way through a stormy situation.

James then proceeds to tell us that the tongue can bless people like a *fountain*. What a beautiful picture of the Spirit-filled ministry! It reminds us of the words of the Lord Jesus who said, "Out of his heart will flow rivers of living water" (John 7:38). All around us are thirsty men and women who need the water of life, and unless we open our mouths to speak out of the abundance of our hearts, how are people going to come to life in Jesus Christ?

But James hasn't finished. The tongue is not only like a fountain, but also like a *tree*. Solomon expresses the same idea when he says that "a wholesome tongue is a tree of life, but perverseness in it breaks the spirit" (Prov. 15:4). And David tells us that the blessed man is "like a tree planted by the rivers of water, that brings forth its fruit in its season, whose leaf also shall not wither; and whatever he does shall prosper" (Ps. 1:3). What a portrait of a witnessing Christian!

He speaks with *authority* because he is like "a tree planted by the rivers of water." His roots go deeply into the revelation of the Word of God and the resources of the Holy Spirit. His message is never a question of human speculation, but rather of divine declaration; he speaks with authority.

He speaks with *propriety* because he brings "forth [his] fruit in [his] season" (Ps. 1:3). There is not only fruitfulness in his content, but fitness in his challenge. The Christian should be the first to speak against the wrongs and evils of the day. His mandate is ever to "Preach the word. . . . Convince, rebuke, exhort, with all longsuffering and teaching" (2 Tim. 4:2).

He speaks with *vitality* because his "leaf also shall not wither" (Ps. 1:3). There is nothing dead or boring when he utters the word of truth. Like an evergreen tree he is perennially fresh. When he utters the word of truth there is life, love, and light in every word.

And then he speaks with *fidelity*, for "whatever he does shall prosper" (Ps. 1:3). Such a man has no doubt as to the results of his personal witness or his public declarations. He knows that the Word of God which goes out of his mouth "shall accomplish what [God pleases], and it shall prosper in the thing for which [God] sent it" (Is. 55:11). Isn't it significant that it is recorded that "the fruit of the righteous is a tree of life, and he who wins souls is wise" (Prov. 11:30)?

How true are the words that "death and life are in the power of the tongue!" (Prov. 18:21). May God ever enable us to minister *life* instead of death.

In some small measure, then, we have examined what Solomon means when he says, "There is . . . a time to keep silence, and a time to speak" (Eccl. 3:1, 7). How important it is, therefore, to know not only of the mastery of the tongue, but also of the ministry of the tongue, for we will never know when we will speak our last word on earth.

A young man had cancer of the tongue. Only by removing the tongue could his life be saved. Before the operation the doctor said, "If there is anything you want to say, say it now, for these will be the last words you ever speak!" After thinking a minute, the young man exclaimed, "Thank God for Jesus Christ!" Lovely last words! (Choice Gleanings Calendar 1977).

Remember, we communicate either by silence or by speech. Oh, that these tongues of ours would ever bring praise and glory to our Lord and Savior Jesus Christ!

Think on These Things (Phil. 4:8)

As a chaplain in the Second World War, I was stationed in Newport, South Wales. The hardest task I had to perform was to preach to the troops as they boarded the ships to storm the Dunkirk beaches. I knew that most of these precious young men would never return. The verse that nerved me to be clear, concise, and courageous in presenting the gospel was Proverbs 18:21, "Death and life are in the power of the tongue." It was certainly not the time to be silent. Souls were at stake and eternal issues had to be faced. This was wartime pressure, but I wonder if peacetime leisure is any less compelling for you and me?

14

A Time to Love
And a Time to Hate

The two greatest forces in the universe are love and hate. When wrongly diverted they can desecrate life, but when rightly directed they can consecrate life. It is imperative that we interpret these two qualities of love and hate in the light of our Lord's teaching, in order that we would love as He would love and hate as He would hate.

The first thing that we shall discover is that when we truly love we fulfill:

Life's Total Obligation

When a lawyer asked our Lord what commandment was the greatest in the law of God, Jesus quoted the Old Testament (Deut. 6:4; Lev. 19:18) and declared:

135

The first of all the commandments is: "Hear, O Israel, the Lord our God, the Lord is one. And you shall love the Lord your God with all your heart, with all your soul, with all your mind, and with all your strength." This is the first commandment. And the second, like it, is this: "You shall love your neighbor as yourself." There is no other commandment greater than these. (Mark 12:29–31)

According to rabbinical teaching, there were 613 precepts in the Law. Of this considerable number all could not be observed. For this reason some of the religious leaders taught that if a man rightly selected some great precept to obey, he might safely disregard the rest of the Law. This is the kind of doctrine against which James expostulated when he wrote, "Whoever shall keep the whole law, and yet stumble in one point, he is guilty of all" (James 2:10). So we see both the importance and significance of the Master's reply to the lawyer's question. He not only gave the answer to life's greatest question, but also spelled out life's total obligation. In a word, it is love to God and love to man.

First, then, *love to God*—"You shall love the Lord your God with all your heart, with all your soul, with all your mind, and with all your strength" (Mark 12:30). A. W. Tozer rightly reminds us that:

God being who He is must always be sought for Himself, never as a means toward something else. Whoever seeks other objects and not God is on his own; he may obtain those objects if he is able, but he will never have God. God is never found accidentally. "Ye shall seek me, and find me, when ye shall search for me with all your heart" [Jer. 29:13] . . . The teaching of the Bible is that God is Himself the end for which man was created. "Whom have I in heaven but thee [Ps. 73:25]." The first and greatest commandment is to love God with every power of our entire being. Where love like that exists there can be no place for a second object. If we love God as much as we should, surely we cannot dream of a loved object beyond Him that He might help us to obtain. (1962)

Bernard of Clairvaux begins his radiant little treatise on the love of God with a question and an answer. The question, Why should we love God? The answer, Because He is God. He develops the idea further, but for the enlightened heart little more need be said. We should love God because He is God. Beyond this the angels cannot think.

With this in mind, we need to examine the words our Savior used to describe the measure of our love. He said, "You shall love the Lord your God with all your heart, with all your soul, with all your mind, and with all your strength" (Mark 12:30). While it is difficult to define with any finality the significance of each of these terms used, it is still important to emphasize that God intends us to love Him with every part of our being.

St. Bernard says, "The measure of our love to God is to love Him without measure; for the immense goodness of God deserves all the love that we can possibly give to Him" (Spence and Exell 1975, 16:157).

For practical purposes, this means *we must love God with a real love*—"You shall love the Lord your God with all your heart" (Mark 12:30). Among the Hebrews, the heart was considered to be the seat of the understanding, the home of the affections, and the center of the will. This describes the intellectual, emotional, and volitional outgoing of love to God. Such response is reflective of reality. In this day of play acting we need to challenge ourselves as to whether we really love God. It was to religious people that Jesus said, "This people honors Me with their lips, but their heart is far from Me" (Mark 7:6). Has it ever occurred to you that more lies are said, or sung, during the hours of worship on a Sunday than possibly any other time of the week? We stand up and sing, "Take my life, and let it be consecrated, Lord, to Thee," and quite frankly, it's a lie; for, if we really meant it, our Christian behavior and service would be different.

During the Napoleonic Wars the emperors of Prussia, Austria, and Russia were discussing the unquestioning obedience of their soldiers. They agreed that each would call in his sentinel and command him to leap out of a second-story window. First, the Prussian monarch gave the drastic order. "Your majesty, it would kill me," his bodyguard complained. He was dismissed, and the Austrian soldier was subjected to the same test. "I'll do it," he said, "if you really mean what you say." Then the Czar gave his man the same order, and the officer immediately started to obey. But he was stopped as he put one leg over the window ledge. Were these sovereigns really plotting murder? No, *their purpose was not to sacrifice their soldiers, but to test their obedience!* Are we so loyal to Christ that to obey His will is our chief delight? Do we love Him with all our heart? (Bosch 1976).

We must love God with an intense love—"You shall love the Lord your God with all your . . . soul" (Mark 12:30). This means all the living powers of our personality. This intensity of love can be illustrated at many levels. Just watch "the way of a man with a virgin" (Prov. 30:19). Look at the facial expressions of an audience viewing a human-interest movie. Sit with a crowd during an exciting game of football, or tennis, and so on. Quite honestly it makes me mad when I hear the critics deride the passion with which I preach or share my faith, and yet see these same individuals express similar intensity of emotion in relational situations of lesser importance. I do not believe that anyone can love God with all his or her soul without showing it and sharing it. I agree with A. T. Pierson who once said, "A light that does not shine, a germ that does not grow, a spring that does not flow, is no more of an anomaly than a Christian who does not witness."

We must love God with a discerning love—"You shall love the Lord your God with all your . . . mind" (Mark 12:30). The emphasis here is more on the intellectual powers. The Bible is so balanced in its presentation of truth. While our love to God must be emotional—to be love at all—it also must be intellectual. This thought is undoubtedly implied when the apostle Paul writes, "I beseech you therefore, brethren, by the mercies of God, that you present your bodies a living sacrifice, holy, acceptable to God, which is your *reasonable service* [or intellectual service]" (Rom. 12:1). W. E. Vine aptly explains this verse by stating, "The sacrifice is to be intelligent, in contrast to those offered by ritual and compulsion; the presentation is to be in accordance with the spiritual intelligence of those who are new creatures in Christ and are mindful of 'the mercies of God'" (1961, 3:253). Nobody can study the Scriptures with any perceptiveness without concluding that in the reckoning of God *the mind* matters. In the divine purpose and instructions, the burnt offering was to be laid on the altar, piece by piece, with thoughtfulness and deliberation. Our whole mental processes are to be involved when we surrender our lives to Christ.

General Charles G. Gordon was an outstanding man of God. When the British government sought to reward him for his brilliant service in China, he declined all money and titles but accepted a gold medal inscribed with the record of his thirty-three engagements. It was his most prized possession. But after his death the medal could not be found. Eventually it was learned that he had sent it to Manchester during a severe famine, directing that it should be melted down and used to buy bread for the poor. Under the date of its sending, these words were found written in his diary, "The last earthly thing I had in this world that I valued I have given to the Lord Jesus Christ" (Naismith 1962, 80[457]). His love for the Savior had constrained him to relinquish his one treasured possession for the relief of the destitute. He would not cling to earthly honor, but casting its last vestige aside, he sought only to serve the Master for the gospel's sake. Here was a man whose consecration to Christ was an evidence of loving thought.

We must love God with an active love—"You shall love the Lord your God with all your . . . strength" (Mark 12:30). Quite obviously, the physical powers are implied here. This means the deliberate involvement and employment of all our faculties. The response of our love can never be complete unless we can look into the face of our Lord and Master and say, "Think through my mind, speak through my lips, work through my hands, walk through my feet, and radiate through my personality."

I have always been impressed with the range of teaching that we find in the New Testament on the physical body. Indeed, it is a subject all its own. Suffice it to say, however, Paul, in particular, teaches that the body is to be surrendered (Rom. 12:1–2), exercised (1 Tim. 4:8), disciplined (1 Cor. 9:27), preserved (1 Thess. 5:23), and employed (1 Cor. 6:20). What is more, when we stand before the judgment seat of Christ we are going to be judged for things done in the *body*, whether they be good or bad (2 Cor. 5:10). Moreover, this teaching comes alive when we realize that Christ depends on your body and mine in order to express His life here upon earth. He is the Head, but we are the Body, and our obligation to God is not fulfilled unless we love Him with all our strength.

So there is a time to love, and that "time" spans our entire earthly existence and beyond, as we live for God and His glory.

But then there is the second commandment: *love to man*— "Love your neighbor as yourself" (Mark 12:31). It is important to notice that this second commandment is likened to the first; that is to say, in nature and extent. It represents the total obligation of man to man. The verb here as well as in the first commandment, implies not merely animal or worldly affection, but love from the highest moral considerations without self-interest. Moreover, the word "neighbor" in this verse means everyone with whom we are concerned. Man is to be loved because he is in God's image and likeness, and therefore heir of the same hope as us.

John the apostle says, "This commandment we have from Him: that he who loves God must love his brother also" (1 John 4:21). And, of course, we have our Lord's words, "Whatever you want men to do to you, do also to them" (Matt. 7:12). Paul also helps us to interpret our love to man in practical terms when he says, "So husbands ought to love their own wives as their own bodies; he who loves his wife loves himself. For no one ever hated his own flesh, but nourishes and cherishes it" (Eph. 5:28–29).

It follows, therefore, that to love our neighbor as ourselves is to nourish and cherish our fellow man. In practical terms, this means *a caring love for our neighbor.* One of the problems of our modern way of life is the insensitivity and indifference that prevail in human relationships.

In the 1890's, Julia Ward Howe asked a United States senator to help liberate an African American from a desperate situation. The legislator exclaimed, "Madam, I'm so busy with plans for *the benefit of the whole race* that I have *no time to help individuals!*" Angered by his lack of compassion, Mrs. Howe replied, "I'm glad our Lord never displayed such a calloused attitude" (Bosch 1976). You and I know that He always sought out the individual who was in need.

One great example that illustrates the importance of an individual is given in our Lord's story of the Good Samaritan (Luke 10:25–37). You will remember that he related this tale in order to answer the specific question, "Who is my neighbor?" And the answer, of course, was the man who fell among thieves, was stripped of his clothes and wounded, and was left half dead. The priest and Levite who passed by both shrank from the trouble and expense of meddling with the poor victim of the robbers. Perhaps a cowardly fear of being identified with a holdup was mixed with these feelings; but notwithstanding this, their conduct was inhuman and unpardonable, even though it was natural. Alas, this whole attitude faithfully portrays the lovelessness of multitudes of men and women professing Christianity today. With the Samaritan, however, it was different. We read that he came to where the dying man was, and "when he saw him, he had compassion" (Luke 10:33). That is *caring* love.

But with the caring love, there must also be *a sharing love for our neighbor*. When we think of love we tend to become "all talk and no action." But again, that is not *agape* love. The apostle John says: "Whoever has this world's goods, and sees his brother in need, and shuts up his heart from him, how does the love [the noun, *agape*] of God abide in him? My little children, let us not love [the verb, *agapao*] in word or in tongue, but in deed and in truth" (1 John 3:17–18).

The Good Samaritan was not satisfied with feeling sorry for the beaten up man; he did something about it. The story tells us that "he went to him and bandaged his wounds, pouring on oil and wine; and he set him on his own animal, brought him to an inn, and took care of him. On the next day, when he departed, he took out two denarii, gave them to the innkeeper, and said to him, 'Take care of him; and whatever more you spend, when I come again, I will repay you' " (Luke 10:34–35). All these tender little details of the Samaritan's compassionate love are sketched in by a Master-hand.

Without even developing the practical aspects of this sharing love, we note that there was medical attention, transportation, hospitality, and follow-up. That is action! That is sharing love! No wonder Jesus added, "Go and do likewise" (Luke 10:37).

The story is told about "a small boy who came from a poor home. He was shabbily dressed and his clothes were patched. Although he liked all of his teachers at school, one of them was a special favorite. When asked why, he simply replied, 'She's so interested in me, she doesn't seem to see my patches.'

That's the way . . . believers look at others when they're really 'loving for Jesus!'"

> May I be loving, no matter the cost,
> Showing compassion to all who have need;
> Willing to aid both the saved and the lost,
> This, blessed Savior, I earnestly plead!
>
> Anonymous

So the Preacher says, "There is . . . a time to love" (Eccl. 3:1, 8). I must add that there is no limit to that time, for love never fails.

But there is also a time to hate, and that brings us to:

Life's Total Opposition

Now we must recognize right away that the word "hate" in Scripture is used in various ways. In some contexts it is employed maliciously, in others, relatively, and yet again in others, absolutely. Malicious hatred, even under the most aggravated personal provocation, is forbidden. Jesus said, "Whoever is angry with his brother without a cause shall be in danger of the judgment" (Matt. 5:22). And John adds, "He who hates his brother is in darkness" (1 John 2:11); and moreover, "Whoever hates his brother is a murderer" (1 John 3:15).

Relative hatred really means "to love less." When God says, "Jacob I have loved, but Esau I have hated" (Rom. 9:13), he is speaking relatively of what He saw in those two persons. Naturally speaking, Esau was a nobler man, but he was destitute of faith. He despised the birthright because it was a thing of spiritual value and required faith to apprehend it. On the other hand, Jacob, though carnal and crooked, had the faith to desire the spiritual birthright and become the Israel of God.

Another example of relative hatred is found in the words of Jesus when He said, "If anyone comes to Me and does not hate his father and mother, wife and children, brothers and sisters, yes, and his own life also, he cannot be My disciple"

(Luke 14:26). What the Master was teaching was that natural affection, when compared with a Christian's devotedness to Christ, appears to be nothing more than hatred. Only when these natural affections are sanctified and sublimated by the Spirit of God can they rise to the level of divine love.

But our concern in this study has to do with absolute hatred. It can be, therefore, admissible only in a relationship to God, which constrains us to count His enemies as ours. And this inevitably brings us to life's total opposition. As people of God, we are totally opposed to sin. This means *we are to hate sin*. David could avow, "I hate every false way" (Ps. 119:128). Quite simply, we are called upon to hate everything that God hates. While the list is by no means comprehensive, Solomon helps us to understand what God hates when he says, "These six things the Lord hates, yes, seven are an abomination to Him: a proud look, a lying tongue, hands that shed innocent blood, a heart that devises wicked plans, feet that are swift in running to evil, a false witness who speaks lies, and one who sows discord among brethren" (Prov. 6:16–19). Let us look at these seven objects of God's hatred.

There is ***the proud look***. Pride is the sin that expelled Lucifer from the place of God's throne. Pride is the sin that drove Adam and Eve from the paradise of Eden. Pride is the sin that will keep men and women out of heaven, because it keeps them from coming to Christ. James tells us that "God resists the proud, but gives grace to the humble" (James 4:6). That is a frightening statement. It literally means that an omnipotent God sets Himself up against a proud person until he learns with Nebuchadnezzar that "those who walk in pride He is able to put down" (Dan. 4:37). For that ancient king, unbroken pride involved seven years of insanity.

There is ***the lying tongue***. The devil is described as the father of lies (John 8:44), and one day, through the Antichrist, he will persuade the world to "believe the lie" (2 Thess. 2:11). So any form of lying is complicity with the devil himself. We live in a day when lying is a virtual lifestyle. I see it in play-acting, we view it in advertisements, and we hear it in excesses and exaggerations of modern speech. Let us remember God hates the lying tongue.

There are *the bloody hands.* In our country we are told that if all the statistics were recorded we could report the rate of a murder a minute. The situation is so serious that we have become prisoners in our own homes! But we must remember that in God's book a murderous thought is seen as a murderous act. As I have pointed out already, "Whoever hates his brother is a murderer, and you know that no murderer has eternal life abiding in him" (1 John 3:15).

There is *the malicious heart.* Some people never seem to be satisfied unless they are intent on some mischief. And this is by no means confined to the muggers and punks on the street. A malicious heart can be found in the home, in the church, and in the office. It is the very opposite of the *agape* love which thinks no evil and rejoices not in iniquity (1 Cor. 13:5–6).

There are *the wayward feet.* Man was created to walk with God, but he has chosen, like a straying sheep, to go his own way. This departure from the highway of holiness is an affront to God. No one can turn his back on the Lord without running into mischief. Indeed, we are warned, "there is a way that seems right to a man, but its end is the way of death" (Prov. 14:12).

There are *the deceptive lips.* These lips are closely related to the lying tongue. The matter of deception, however, is of such serious moment that the Spirit of God has underscored it twice for our learning. Has it ever occurred to you how often we misrepresent the truth in our prayers, our songs, and our testimonies? God hates this, and so must we.

There is *the spirit of discord.* This is the last of the abominations in this list. Perhaps there is nothing that has nullified the witness of the church of Jesus Christ like the factions and divisions that abound in the religious world of our day.

I personally believe this brings more heartache to our Savior than any other sin that you and I can commit. In His last recorded prayer before Calvary, He cried, "that they all may be one, as You Father, are in Me, and I in You; that they also may be one in Us, that the world may believe that You sent Me" (John 17:21). Every time we sow discord we negate the spirit and words of that prayer.

Now let us face it; these seven sins are an abomination; God hates them, and we are to hate them. Sin not only deserves, but also demands our total opposition.

We conclude, then, that there is "a time to love, and a time to hate," and in the light of all that we have considered, two aspects of Christian commitment are called for: one is life's obligation to God and man, and the other is life's opposition to sin and evil. The Bible says, "Abhor what is evil. Cling to what is good" (Rom. 12:9). Commenting on this verse, Dr. Graham Scroggie (1952, 84) writes, "True love is not present where there is not a moral recoil from evil." May the Holy Spirit enable us to hate sin as fervently as we love God.

Think on These Things (Phil. 4:8)

God's standard of love is so high that none of us can attain unto it. How grateful, therefore, we ought to be to know and experience that divine love by the power of the indwelling Spirit! And we read that "the fruit of the Spirit is love" (Gal. 5:22). Commenting on this verse D. L. Moody (Wirt and Beckstrom 1974, 148) notes that "joy is love exalted; peace is love in repose; long-suffering is love enduring; gentleness is love in society; goodness is love in action; faith is love on the battlefield; meekness is love in school; and temperance (self-control) is love in training."

15

A Time of War
And A Time of Peace

*W*hen General Douglas MacArthur died, the United States lost one of its greatest generals and noblest sons. Writing about his background, one weekly magazine aptly said that MacArthur was "born to battle." His life accordingly was molded and matured amid the perils and hardships of war.

It can be equally said that the Christian has been "born to battle." While this warfare is carried on in a different sphere, it is nevertheless a battle. It is a battle against self, sin, and Satan himself; and in this encounter we are asked to "fight the good fight of faith" (1 Tim. 6:12) and to "endure hardship as a good soldier of Jesus Christ" (2 Tim. 2:3) (Prairie Bible Institute 1964, 206). There is a very close connection between the previous couplet and the one we are about to consider. When we love God and hate sin, we virtually declare war on the devil. Of course, as victories are won, there is always the blessing of peace. So, there is a time of war and a time of peace as long as life endures. Through all the Bible, and particularly in the New Testament, the Christian life is likened to a fight.

But with the fight, there is also the reward of peace. The apostle Paul could say at the end of his life, "I have fought the good fight, I have finished the race, I have kept the faith. Finally, there is laid up for me the crown of righteousness, which the Lord, the righteous Judge, will give to me on that Day, and not to me only but also to all who have loved His appearing" (2 Tim. 4:7–8). We must face then:

The Call to Battle

The Puritan, Charles Bridges (1960, 62–63), points out that a time of war may arise from man's ungoverned passions (James 4:1), the just reparation of injury (Gen. 14:14–17), or some legitimate occasion of self defense (2 Sam. 10:3–6). But he adds,

> All this is not chance. It is the providence or permissive control of the Great Ruler of the universe. *War* is his chastisement; peace his returning blessing. It is his prerogative to 'make *wars* to cease unto the ends of the earth' (Ps. 46:9) to 'scatter . . . the people that delight in war' (Ps. 68:30); and, when the sword has done its appointed work, to 'make *peace* in the borders of his people' (Ps. 147:14).

This is certainly a helpful analysis of the biblical treatment of war and peace.

But our concern in this chapter will focus entirely on the Christian warfare. In the Book of the Revelation we read about war in heaven, when "the great dragon was cast out, that serpent of old, called the Devil" (Rev. 12:9). The strategy of that great victory is then explained as John the apostle goes on to say that "they overcame him by the blood of the Lamb and by the word of their testimony, and they did not love their lives to the death" (Rev. 12:11).

Among other things, we can learn two important secrets on how to wage this holy war against the devil. First, *how to detect the devil.* "The great dragon was cast out, that serpent of old, called the Devil and Satan, who deceives the whole world; he was cast to the earth, and his angels were cast out with him" (Rev. 12:9). With the instruction we find in the Holy Scriptures and the illumination we derive from the Holy Spirit we can learn how to detect the devil by studying his titles and tactics.

Consider *the titles of the devil.* In that one statement we have four names, or titles, which describe this archenemy of men and women. He is called "the great dragon" because he is essentially a destroyer. Peter even speaks of him as "a roaring lion, seeking whom he may devour" (1 Pet. 5:8). He is called "that old *serpent*" because he is a deceiver. His subtlety and seductions are unmatched by any other creature in the universe. He is called "the devil" because he is a slanderer and an accuser. And then he is called "Satan" because he is an opposer of all that is holy, just, and good. What an insight this gives us into the names and nature of this supernatural personality we call the devil.

But, then, examine carefully *the tactics of the devil.* We read that he "deceives the whole world" (Rev. 12:9); and again, he is "the accuser of our brethren" (Rev. 12:10). Here is his strategy spelled out in two words—deception and accusation. With supernatural subtlety he can deceive anyone into rebelling against God. And then having achieved this, he accuses his victim until he destroys the total personality. The reason people try to drown their guilt and fears in harmful, or even harmless, preoccupations is because of the relentless accusations of the devil.

This does not excuse man's accountability for sinning against God, but it does explain the consequences that follow

when man rebels against Him. So by understanding these titles and tactics of the devil we can detect not only His presence and power, but also His purpose in the world today.

I am glad, however, that the Bible takes us further and
shows us not only how to detect the devil, but also *how to defeat
the devil.* "And they overcame him by the blood of the Lamb
and by the word of their testimony, and they did not love their
lives to the death" (Rev. 12:11). In this one verse we have a
threefold strategy for overcoming Satan himself. In simple language, let me put it this way. *We overcome the devil by the blood of
Christ.* When Jesus Christ died on the cross as the Lamb of
God, He made possible the conquest of the devil in our everyday lives. The Bible tells us that when Christ hung upon that
cruel tree He "disarmed principalities and powers, [making] a
public spectacle of them, triumphing over them in it" (Col.
2:15). And in another place we read that "through death He
might destroy him who had the power of death, that is, the
devil" (Heb. 2:14). The meaning of these verses is that in His
death Jesus nullified the power of Satan to triumph over any
person who knows the redeeming and protecting power of His
precious blood. While the devil is still alive and loose on the
earth, his final doom was sealed when Jesus died on the cross
and rose again from the dead. In fact, as He anticipated Calvary, our Savior declared, "Now is the judgment of this world;
now the ruler of this world will be cast out" (John 12:31). On the
basis of that statement alone, you and I can experience victory
over the devil. He knows that his power to defeat the child of
God has been annulled through the cross of Christ. When we
remind our enemy of Calvary, *there is always victory.*

We overcome the devil by the word of Christ. The only testimony that counts is that which is rooted in the Holy Scriptures, and there is power in the Word of God to overcome the
devil. This is dramatically shown in our Lord's temptation in
the wilderness (Matt. 4:1–11). You will remember how the
devil attacked Him three times, and on each occasion He

overcame by the word of His testimony. He could say, "It is written," "It is written," "It is written." How true it is that the sword of the Spirit is the Word of God (Eph. 6:17). How important it is, therefore, that we should spend much time in the Holy Scriptures, in order that we might be able to draw the sword whenever we are attacked.

We overcome the devil by the Spirit of Christ. There is only one power that can make us resist, even unto death, and that is the power of the Holy Spirit. When our Lord confronted Satan in the wilderness He was *"driven* by the Spirit." When He fought the battle at Calvary He did it through the power of "the eternal Spirit" (Heb. 9:14). Isaiah reminds us, "when the enemy comes in like a flood, the Spirit of the LORD will lift up a standard against him" (Is. 59:19).

In Jesus Christ, we have this threefold power to overcome the devil: the power of the blood, the power of the Word, and the power of the Spirit.

Some time ago I was in Norfolk, Virginia, where I saw for the first time a large, nuclear-powered aircraft carrier, the Nimitz, named after Admiral Chester Nimitz. Its overall length is 1,092 feet, and its flight deck is about 4.5 acres. Its combat load displacement is about 95,000 tons, it carries a crew of 6,286 persons and has a speed of over 30 knots. One of its significant features is that because of nuclear propulsion it can run for 13 years before refueling. In many ways it is like a floating city, containing everything a community of over 6,000 would require. Fighter planes can take off and land, at the same time, even at full speed. The ship contains the most sophisticated electronic equipment for all purposes of peace and war. The thing I learned about this remarkable carrier is that it is totally unarmed! It has no mounted guns or missile-launchers. On its own it is totally vulnerable to enemy attack. But that is not the whole story. When in action, this ship is protected by subs under the sea, destroyers on the sea, and aircraft above the sea— and this constitutes the total protection needed by the carrier.

As I recalled these facts, I couldn't help relating that whole operation to the text that we have been considering. The submarines answer to the blood of Christ, the destroyers answer to the Word of Christ, and the planes answer to the Spirit of Christ. In and of ourselves, we are totally vulnerable to the attacks of the enemy, but God has not sent us out as carriers of the gospel without adequate protection. We have our submarines, our destroyers, and our aircraft! In the holy war in which we are engaged we can be more than conquerors. Hallelujah! In the spirit of this victory, we can with confidence now appropriate:

The Calm of Blessing

With the time of war, the Preacher promises "a time of peace." In the Scriptures, the word "peace" has reference to health, prosperity, well being, security, and respite from war. Isaiah reminds us that "there is no peace . . . for the wicked" (Is. 48:22; 57:21), even though many of the wicked will continue to seek to encourage themselves with a false peace. For the Christian, however, the word "peace" gathers up the innumerable blessings that are found in the gospel of the grace of God, and these blessings are not benefits laid up in eternal glory *only*, but are a present experience.

Think, first of all, of *the individual peace that we can possess* (Eph. 2:14). Paul declares that Christ "is our peace." And the Master confirmed this when He said: "Peace I leave with you, My peace I give to you; not as the world gives do I give to you. Let not your heart be troubled, neither let it be afraid" (John 14:27). What the world gives, it takes away again; what Jesus gives lasts forever.

Now the Bible has much to say on this individual peace. We read, for instance, that this peace is from God. In many of the apostolic greetings we have the phrase "peace from God" (Col. 1:2; 1 Thess. 1:1). The obvious inference is that God is the Source of all true peace. Indeed, He is spoken of as "the

God of peace" (Heb. 13:20). How foolish it is for man to imagine that he can create peace outside of God. With all the good intentions of presidents and politicians in the world, there will be no permanent peace until Jesus Christ, the Prince of Peace, is owned and obeyed. As William M. Peck has put it, "There will be no peace so long as God remains unseated at the conference tables" (Wirt and Beckstrom 1974, 170 [2300]).

Then the Bible speaks of "peace with God" (Rom. 5:1). This is the work of Christ into which the individual enters by faith. Because of His death on the cross, all the righteous demands of a holy God against sin have been duly met. Therefore, you and I can know this state of peace through simple faith. And the wonderful thing about it is that no devil in hell, no man on earth, no angel in heaven, can ever rob us of this peace with God. Whereas we were once at enmity with God, and war prevailed, now all hostilities have ceased and peace prevails.

The Bible also speaks of "the peace *of* God" (Phil. 4:7). This is the inward state of the soul of the believer who, having entered into peace with God through faith in Christ, has committed to God, through prayer and supplication, all his anxieties. This peace is described as passing all understanding. It remains unshaken and unruffled in the depths of our heart. J. D. Mozley says:

> "You have seen the sea when it was perfectly smooth, with hardly a ripple on the water; and you have [also] watched when it was lashed in fury by the tempest. But you know, all this rage of the elements is only on the surface; below the waves and foam and howling winds there are depths which no storm can ever reach. Such is the contrast between the outward trials of life and the deep inward peace that reigns in the heart which is stayed on God. We cannot escape the trials of

life, but if there be within us this true trust in God, then there will be depth in our inmost being where no storms can reach and where all is calm and still" (1957, 331).

Thus peace is "a conception distinctly peculiar to Christianity, the tranquil state of a soul assured of its salvation through Christ, and so fearing nothing from God, and content with its earthly lot of whatever sort it is" (Feinberg 1960).

But with the individual peace that we are to possess, there is the *universal peace that we can promote*. Writing to believers, Paul says, "As much as depends on you, live peaceably with all men" (Rom. 12:18). And Jesus said, "Blessed are the peacemakers, for they shall be called sons of God" (Matt. 5:9). With the entrance of sin into the world there came the need for a peacemaker, for wherever there are peace breakers there must be peacemakers. And so the Lord Jesus came and died and rose again, not only to make peace by the blood of His cross, but also to share this peace through you and me.

We are to promote peace within the church. The word to each one of us is "endeavoring to keep the unity of the Spirit in the bond of peace" (Eph. 4:3). Now as we have seen, peace is God's gift to His own people. But once we possess this gift we are to promote it by walking "worthy of the calling with which [we] were called" (Eph. 4:1). We are to allow the Lord Jesus, who is indwelling Peace, to speak, live, look, and love through our lives within the local church. There is nothing that brings joy to the heart of the Lord more than a united church. "Behold, how good and how pleasant it is for brethren to dwell together in unity!" (Ps. 133:1). By the same token, there is nothing that grieves the divine heart more than a divided church. I believe His prayer every day is, "Father, make them all one, 'as You Father, are in Me, and I in you; that they also may be one in Us, that the world may believe that You sent Me'" (John 17:21).

But the promotion of peace goes beyond the church to the world. We are exhorted to pray "for kings and all who are in authority, that we may lead a quiet and peaceable life in all godliness and reverence, for this is good and acceptable in the sight of God our Savior, who desires all men to be saved and to come to the knowledge of the truth" (1 Tim. 2:2–4). This is the greatest contribution we can ever make to a measure of world peace. Such a discipline as this does not commend itself to the carnal mind, and far less to the natural man—who would rather try to organize peace in the energy of the flesh. But history is replete with examples of how God has brought tranquility and peace into national situations because of the prayers of God's people.

We are also to "preach the gospel of peace" (Rom. 10:15). Even though the world does not know it, and in many cases would not accept it, the greatest promoters and purveyors of peace are the despised evangelists and pastors. Since peace can never come until men are right with God, there is nothing more worthwhile or valuable in the world in which we live than the preaching of "the gospel of peace."

It is true, of course, that universal peace will never be experienced until Jesus Christ comes to reign as the Prince of Peace. God hasten that day! In the meantime, however, the greatest measure of peace we shall know upon this planet is when our lives are yielded to the only One who made peace and is our Peace, even the Lord Jesus Christ.

The Chinese have a proverb that goes like this: "If there is righteousness in the heart, there will be beauty in the character. If there is beauty in the character, there will be harmony in the home. If there is harmony in the home, there will be order in the nation. When there is order in the nation, there will be peace in the world."

We have seen, then, that there is "a time of war, and a time of peace." How wonderful to know that in Jesus we can have victory in war and liberty in peace, because in every situation He is the contemporary Christ!

Think on These Things (Phil. 4:8)

As long as we remain in this sin-cursed world, there will be "wars and rumors of wars" (Matt. 24:6). Now and again there will be an unsettled "peace." Only when the Prince of Peace is enthroned will wars cease and peace prevail. In the meantime, for the surrendered Christian there can be victory and harmony in daily living. In the language of the apostle Paul we can exclaim, "Thanks be to God, who gives us the victory through our Lord Jesus Christ" (1 Cor. 15:57). Commenting on this doxology Dr. Leon Morris ([1958] 1976, 235) writes: "The use of the present participle may convey the thought that it is God's characteristic to give victory. There is also the implication that we participate in that victory *now*, and that we participate in it *daily*."

Conclusion

The *song* that we have expounded line upon line is really a prelude to the *sermon* that makes up the rest of Ecclesiastes. Presently we hear the "Preacher" say: "Let us hear the conclusion of the whole matter:

> Fear God and keep His commandments,
> For this is man's all.
> For God will bring every work into judgment,
> Including every secret thing,
> Whether good or evil" (Eccl. 12:13–14)

In effect, he is telling us to face up to the *truth* he has introduced in his "Song of Life." Like a good preacher he structures the sermon that follows with precision and conviction. He gives us his text, his theme, and the thrust of his sermon.

Look at the *text* of the sermon—"Vanity of vanities, all is vanity" (Eccl. 1:2). With that as a starter Solomon goes right through the book with this one note sounding out again and again. He speaks of the life of vanity or emptiness thirty-seven times. As far as he is concerned, man and nature move in a cycle of endless repetition and monotony.

Then the preacher develops the *theme* of the sermon. Covering more than ten areas of life he shows that life without God is futile and hopeless. For example, he speaks of *the emptiness of human knowledge*. He says, "I set my heart to know wisdom and to know madness and folly. I perceived that this also is grasping for the wind. For in much wisdom is much grief, and he who increases knowledge increases sorrow" (Eccl. 1:17–18). Solomon, who was the wisest man who ever lived, (2 Chr. 1:11,12;) applied himself to seek and to search out wisdom. But in his lifetime he found no profit, no enduring satisfaction from all his acquired knowledge. He could recall only, "He who increases knowledge increases sorrow."

Then he turns to *the emptiness of human labor* and asks, "What profit has a man from all his labor in which he toils under the sun?" (Eccl. 1:3). And again, "I looked on all the works that my hands had done and on the labor in which I had toiled; and indeed all was vanity and grasping for the wind. There was no profit under the sun" (Eccl. 2:11). And still again, "For what has man for all his labor, and for the striving of his heart with which he has toiled under the sun? For all his days are sorrowful, and his work burdensome; even in the night his heart takes no rest. This also is vanity" (Eccl. 2:22–23). No one worked harder than Solomon to build a kingdom and to seek fulfillment in his work, but when he had accomplished both his desires and designs, he had to admit that all was vanity.

Once more he cites *the emptiness of human pleasure*. Hear his cynicism, "'Come now, I will test you with mirth; therefore enjoy pleasure'; but surely, this also was vanity. I said of laughter—'Madness!'; and of mirth, 'What does it accomplish?'" (Eccl. 2:1–2). Even his lust for wine, women, and song brought him nothing but emptiness and madness. For him wisdom was vanity, labor was vanity, pleasure was vanity. What a commentary on life! Anyone who imagines that he can experience satisfaction apart from God should peruse this sermon over and over again. It is the most sobering piece of reading to be found in Scripture.

But with the text and theme, the preacher now deals with the *thrust* of his sermon. In the closing verses of Ecclesiastes he writes, "Let us hear the conclusion of the whole matter: Fear God and keep His commandments, for this is man's all. For God will bring every work into judgment, including every secret thing, whether good or evil" (Eccl. 12:13–14). In short, the preacher brings his congregation up with a jolt and cries out: **"It is a time for truth."** And even more important than this, it is time to *respond to the truth*. It is one thing to accept the truth, but it is quite another matter to obey the truth. So the conclusion of the matter is to do something about the truth that we have already received. In practical terms this identifies two tremendous issues that we must all face:

Obedience to the Truth Determines Life's Essential Purpose

"Fear God and keep His commandments" (Eccl. 12:13). In these two statements Solomon sums up for us life's essential purpose. The Westminster Catechism reminds us that "man's chief end is to glorify God and to enjoy Him forever." It follows, therefore, that whatever enables us to do this is the purpose of all truth. Solomon tells us that it is *the worship of God and the service of God.*

It is generally understood that "the fear of the Lord" is an Old Testament phrase for reverential trust and the hatred of evil. It is with such trust and purity in our hearts that we must worship the Lord in the beauty of holiness. This is why David asks, "Who may ascend into the hill of the Lord?" and then answers: "He who has clean hands and a pure heart, who has not lifted up his soul to an idol, nor sworn deceitfully. He shall receive blessing from the Lord, and righteousness from the God of his salvation" (Ps. 24:3–5).

So reverential fear of God is the very essence of worship. Jesus declared, "God is Spirit, and those who worship Him must worship in spirit and truth" (John 4:24). In saying this He made known the twofold secret of worshiping the Father.

First, we need the Holy Spirit to *conduct* us in worship. Only when we are filled with the Holy Spirit can we worship God as we ought. This is why the apostle Paul exhorts us to "be filled with the Spirit, speaking to one another in psalms and hymns and spiritual songs, singing and making melody in your heart to the Lord, giving thanks always for all things to God the Father in the name of our Lord Jesus Christ, submitting to one another in the fear of God" (Eph. 5:18–21).

So we see that whether in speech, song, or silence we cannot truly worship God without being controlled by the Holy Spirit. When you go to worship on a Sunday morning, do you drop on your knees before you ever enter God's house and claim the fullness of the Holy Spirit? If you don't, how can you worship Him in Spirit? The secret of true worship then is to be filled with the Holy Spirit.

But we also need the Holy Scriptures to *instruct* us in worship. We must worship "in . . . truth" (John 4:23). This is why many passages in the Old and New Testament are related entirely to worship. When we worship we are instructed to "present [our] *bodies* a living sacrifice . . . to God" (Rom. 12:1). We cannot understand the true meaning of worship without presenting every faculty of our beings upon the altar of God's acceptance. So Paul says, "I urge you therefore, brethren, by the mercies of God, to present your bodies a living and holy sacrifice acceptable to God, which is your spiritual service of worship" (Rom. 12:1 NASB).

When we worship, we are instructed to present our *praises* as sacrifices to God. "By Him let us continually offer the sacrifice of praise to God, that is, the fruit of our lips, giving thanks to His name" (Heb. 13:15). And with the Psalmist we have to remember that "whoever offers praise glorifies [God]" (Ps. 50:23).

Once again, when we worship we are instructed to present our *money* to God. The Word is clear, "Do not forget to do good and to share, for with such sacrifices God is well pleased" (Heb 13:16). So the apostle Paul says, "Let each one give as he purposes in his heart, not grudgingly or of necessity; for God loves a cheerful giver" (2 Cor. 9:7).

In the three passages that have been quoted, the word "sacrifice" occurs each time. There is the sacrifice of our bodies; that is worship as we dedicate afresh our entire beings to a holy God. There is the sacrifice of our praise; that is when we open our mouths to praise, sing, and exalt our Savior. Then there is the sacrifice of money; that is when we bring that which we have acquired throughout the week and lay it before the Lord as our thank-offering of worship.

But with the worship of God, there is also the *service of God*. "Keep His commandments" (Eccl. 12:13). This injunction comprehends the whole scope of Christian service: in the home, in the church, and in the world. The Word of God makes it plain that each of these areas of life has its own service.

In the home, we are exhorted to submit ourselves one to another in the fear of God—wife to the husband, children to the parents, each one to every one in the Spirit of *agape* love.

In the church, we are exhorted to obey them who have the rule over us and to submit to them as those who must give an account to God (Heb. 13:17). Submission in the church is one of the greatest needs today. And we don't really serve the church unless we know how to submit ourselves to the pastor, to the elders, to the deacons, and to each other within the circle of fellowship—each serving the other, recognizing that the eye cannot say to the nose, "I have no need of you." The ear can't say to the lips, "I have no need of you." The hand can't say to the foot, "I have no need of you" (see 1 Cor. 12:21). We all need each other, and we all serve each other.

Then in the world we are urged to submit ourselves "to every ordinance of man for the Lord's sake" (1 Pet. 2:13). In each instance the word "submission" is used, which implies obedience to the commandment of the Lord.

The highest conception of this submission to the will of the Father is perfectly exemplified in the life of our Lord and

Savior Jesus Christ. All through His life He was constantly saying things like, "I must be about My Father's business" (Luke 2:49), "My food is to do the will of Him who sent Me, and to finish His work" (John 4:34), and "The Son of Man did not come to be served, but to serve, and to give His life a ransom for many" (Matt. 20:28; Mark 10:45). In every sense of the word He was Jehovah's Bondslave.

Then in devoted identification with the Master, Paul could later glory in the fact that he was in turn a bondslave of Jesus Christ. For the Christian, the service of God is nothing less. Are you totally submitted to the good and acceptable and perfect will of God in your home life? Is this true in your church life? In your business life? That is service unto God.

So we have seen that the worship of God and the service of God constitute life's essential purpose. The Lord Jesus made this clear when He declared categorically, "You shall worship the Lord your God, and Him only you shall serve" (Matt. 4:10; Luke 4:8). Let us see to it that we "fear God and keep His commandments" (Eccl. 12:13).

Obedience to the Truth Determines Life's Eternal Prospect

Solomon continues, "For this is man's all. For God will bring every work into judgment, including every secret thing, whether good or evil" (Eccl. 12:13–14). As we have already seen, "man's chief end is to glorify God and enjoy Him forever." This not only affects time, but also eternity. In view of this we ought to live with the values of eternity in view. As Martin Luther put it, "We ought to live as if Christ died yesterday, rose today, and is coming back tomorrow." This, of course, calls for total obedience to the truth of God as it is revealed to us. There are two simple reasons for this.

First, man's personal *fulfillment* depends on obedience to the truth. To "fear God and keep His commandments. For this is man's all" (Eccl. 12:13). That word "all" is a most significant one. It is included by some translators to complete the sense of the sentence; but that is not comprehensive enough. As one scholar has put it, "To fear God and the keep His commandments is not only the whole duty, but the whole honor, the whole interest, and the whole happiness of man." The quest with which the book of Ecclesiastes has been largely concerned is for happiness. But as we have seen already, Solomon did not find it in human knowledge, he did not find it in human labor, he did not find it in human pleasure. Indeed, his conclusion is that life is utterly empty apart from God. But now he states at the end of his sermon that to "fear God and keep His commandments" is to experience true happiness and fulfillment. Jesus taught the same truth in the beatitudes, and the apostle Paul reminds us that "the kingdom of God is not eating and drinking, but righteousness and peace and joy in the Holy Spirit" (Rom. 14:17). So man's present fulfillment depends on obedience to God's truth.

But more than this, man's personal *attainment* depends on obedience to God's truth. "For God will bring every work into judgment, including every secret thing, whether good or evil" (Eccl. 12:14). A British theologian by the name of D. R. Davis once wrote a book entitled *The World We Have Forgotten*. His main thesis was that men and women have become so earth bound and materialistic that they have overlooked the fact that they are creatures of eternity. "Life down here," he says, "is only a prelude to a greater life in the hereafter." So we find the Bible punctuated with announcements and warnings concerning the Day of Judgment. There is a Day of Judgment coming, and we must not forget it. The Bible declares that God "has appointed a day on which He will judge the world in righteousness by the Man whom He has ordained. He has given assurance of this to all by raising Him from the dead" (Acts 17:31). And we are reminded in our text that "God will bring every work into judgment, including every secret thing, whether good or evil." Nothing will be omitted or forgotten, for the Divine Judgment will test everything we have done without partiality. And the sentence will be final.

In the light of this day of reckoning, let us labor that whether present or absent from this life we may be pleasing to him. For we must all appear before the Judgment Seat of Christ. Let us remember the words of the apostle John, "Little children, abide in Him, that when He appears, we may have confidence and not be ashamed before Him at His coming" (1 John 2:28). Also the words of the apostle Paul: "Not that I have already attained, or am already perfected; *but I press on*, that I may lay hold of that for which Christ Jesus has also laid hold of me. Brethren, I do not count myself to have apprehended; but one thing I do, forgetting those things which are behind and reaching forward to those things which are ahead, *I press toward the goal for the prize of the upward call of God in Christ Jesus*" (Phil. 3:12–14).

The motivating thrust throughout this entire book has been that it is **a time for truth.** But this will make no difference in our lives unless *truth* is "mixed with faith" and *obeyed*. So we have learned from the "Preacher's" concluding challenge that obedience to truth determines life's essential purpose, and also life's eternal prospect. What else can we say than to remind ourselves of the little chorus we sometimes sing so glibly:

> Trust and obey,
> For there's *no other way*
> To be happy in Jesus,
> But to trust and obey.
>   John H. Sammis

Select Bibliography

Books

Bridges, Charles. *An Exposition of the Book of Ecclesiastes*. London: Banner of Truth Trust, 1960.

Brunner, Emil. *The Meditator: A Study of the Central Doctrine of the Christian Faith*. Translated by Olive Wyon. London: Lutterworth Press, 1934, 1942.

Chadwick, Samuel. *The Path of Prayer*. Sevenoaks, Kent, England: Hodder and Stoughton Limited, 1934.

Chambers, Oswald. *Shade of His Hand*. Grand Rapids: Discovery House, 1991.

Davies, D. R. *The World We Have Forgotten*. London: The Paternoster Press, 1946.

Delitzsch, Franz. *Commentary on the Song of Songs and Ecclesiastes*. Translated from the German by M.G. Easton. Grand Rapids: Wm. B. Eerdmans Publishing Company, 1900.

Drummond, Henry. *The Greatest Thing in the World*. New York: Word Publishing Company, 1969.

Macaulay, J. C. *Devotional Studies in the Epistle to the Hebrews*. Grand Rapids: Wm. B. Eerdmans Publishing Company, 1948.

Morgan, Edward. *John Elias: Life and Letters*. Edinburg: The Banner of Truth Trust, 1973.

Morris, Leon. *The First Epistle of Paul to the Corinthians: An Introduction and Commentary*. Grand Rapids: Wm. B. Eerdmans Publishing Company, 1958, 9th printing 1976.

Mozley, J. B. *The Biblical Illustrator: Philippians*. Edited by Joseph S. Excell. Grand Rapids: Baker Book House, 1957.

Naismith, A. *1200 Notes Quotes and Anecdotes*. London: Pickering & Inglis Ltd., 1962.

Pollock, John C. *Moody*. Grand Rapids: Zondervan Publishing House, 1963.

Scroggie, W. Graham. *Salvation and Behavior*. London: Pickering & Inglis Ltd., 1952.

Spence, H. D. M. and Exell, Joseph, eds. *The Pulpit Commentary*, 23 vols. Grand Rapids: Wm. B. Eerdmans Publishing Company, 1975.

Tasker, R. V. G. *James*. Leicester: Inter-Varsity Press, 1956.

Tozer, A. W. *Renewed Day by Day: A Daily Devotional*, vol. 1. Compiled by Gerald B. Smith. Camp Hill, Pennsylvania: Christian Publications, 1991.

Vine, W. E. *An Expository Dictionary of New Testament Words*, 11th ed. Old Tappan: Fleming H. Revell Company, 1961.

Wirt, Sherwood Eliot and Beckstrom, Kersten, eds. *Living Quotations for Christians*. New York: Harper & Row, Publishers, Inc., 1974.

Articles

"Anything Goes: Taboos in Twilight" *Newsweek* (November 13, 1967).

"Born to Battle." *The Prairie Overcomer*. Three Hills, Alberta, Canada: Prairie Bible Institute (June 1964).

Bosch, Henry G. *Radio Bible Class*. Grand Rapids: Radio Bible Class (1976).

De Haan, Richard. *Radio Bible Class*. Grand Rapids: Radio Bible Class, (1976).

"Fear of Death." *The Prairie Overcomer.* Three Hills, Alberta, Canada: Prairie Bible Institute (July 1972).

Feinberg, Charles L. "Peace," in *Baker's Dictionary of Theology*, edited by Everett F. Harrison. (Grand Rapids: Baker Book House, 1960).

Johnson, Jack. "Information Age Comes to Television." *Religious Broadcasting* (December 1995).

Miller, J. R. "Comforted," *Come Ye Apart.* Sunbury-on-Thames, England: Thomas Nelson & Sons Limited, 1912.

Morgan, G. Campbell. "The Disciple at Play," in *Discipleship Journal*, 2nd ed. (London: Allenson & Company Ltd., 1934).

Rees, Paul S. "The Service of Silence." *Christianity Today*, (May 10, 1963).

Reid, W. Stanford. "Jesus Christ: Focal Point of Knowledge." *Christianity Today* (May 1968).

Rendall, T. S. "The Sands of Time." *The Prairie Overcomer.* Three Hills, Alberta, Canada: Prairie Bible Institute (January 1964).

Stebbins, Thomas H. "Time: How to Make the 'Nickels and Dimes' Count." *Evangelical Newsletter 2*, 18 (July 4, 1975).

Stone, Marvin. "What are We Planting?" *U.S. News & World Report* (June 1977).

Stott, John R. W. "When Should a Christian Weep?" *Christianity Today* (November 1969).

Tozer, A. W. Tozer. "God Must Be Loved for Himself." *The Alliance Witness* (September 1962).

Miscellaneous Items

Choice Gleanings Calendar (Grand Rapids: Gospel Folio Press, February 21, 1977).

Iverson, Daniel. "Spirit of the Living God." Moody Bible Institute, Chicago, 1935, 1963.

P.O. Box 757800, Memphis, TN 38175-7800 + (901) 757-7977 + Fax: (901) 757-1372 +
www.olford.org + Olford@ixlmemphis.com

OUR HISTORY

The Stephen Olford Center for Biblical Preaching was dedicated on June 4, 1988, in Memphis, Tennessee. It is the international headquarters for Olford Ministries, International and houses the Institute for Biblical Preaching.

The Institute for Biblical Preaching was founded in 1980 to promote biblical preaching and practical training for pastors, evangelists, and lay leaders. After 50 years of pastoral and global ministry, Dr. Olford believes that the ultimate answer to the problems of every age is the anointed expository preaching of God's inerrant Word. It is Dr. Olford's sincere desire that such preaching be restored to contemporary pulpits around the world.

OUR STRATEGY

The purpose of the Institute for Biblical Preaching is to equip and encourage pastors and laymen in expository preaching and exemplary living, so that that the church will be revived and the world will be reached with the saving Word of Christ. The program includes:

- Institutes and special events on expository preaching, pastoral leadership, essentials of evangelism, the fullness of the Holy Spirit, the reality of revival, and other related subjects.
- Workshops for pastors and laymen to preach "live" in order to have their sermons, skills, and styles critiqued constructively.
- 1-Day Video *Institutes* on anointed biblical preaching hosted in churches around the country.
- Consultations on pastoral and practical matters.
- Outreach through wider preaching/teaching ministry, radio broadcasting, literature, audio/video resources, and our internet site.